Continued Praise for
The Impatience Economy

"Augie is an experienced entrepreneur, and his insights on how consumer demands are driving change will be valuable for anyone learning to grow their business faster."

Evan Spiegel, Co-founder and CEO of Snap Inc.

"Patience may be a virtue, but it won't play much of a role in the coming Impatience Economy. Well argued and infectiously optimistic, Augie Fabela's book is a great way to prepare your business for necessary and inevitable change."

Phil Libin, Co-founder of Evernote and
Co-founder and CEO of mmhmm and All Turtles

"The Impatience Economy is real. When was the last time you thought 'way outside the box' about how to deeply connect with your customers? Social Retail Marketing, as defined by Fabela in this book, is the future."

Jerry I. Porras, Professor, Stanford Graduate School of Business

"They say the future is notoriously hard to predict, but Augie Fabela makes it look easy. This book is a field guide for digital and social commerce."

Imran Khan, Founder and CEO of Verishop,
former chief strategy officer of Snap Inc.

"Augie delivers the gold on how to succeed in The Impatience Economy, an era where digital storytelling and commerce will collide and change everything."

Tim Staples, Co-founder and CEO of Shareability,
author of *Break Through the Noise*

"As a strategic business leader and authority on the power of brand, I support our clients through incredibly tough decisions. Augie's insights opened my eyes to the future of industry as we know it. A must-read!"

Michelle Heath, Founder and CEO of Growth Street

"It takes a visionary entrepreneur, like Augie Fabela, who founded one of the largest mobile companies in the world, to see the power and future of Social Retail Marketing."

Mats Granryd, Director General of the GSMA

THE
IMPATIENCE
ECONOMY™

How *Social Retail Marketing*™
Changes Everything

AUGIE K FABELA II

Co-Founder and CEO, FastForward.ai
Co-Founder, Chairman Emeritus, VEON, Ltd.

Published by Redwood Publishing, LLC
Orange County, California
www.redwooddigitalpublishing.com

ISBN 978-1-952106-85-9 (hardcover)
ISBN 978-1-952106-86-6 (paperback)
ISBN 978-1-952106-87-3 (ebook)

Library of Congress Control Number: 2021910989

Although the author and publisher have made every effort to ensure that
the information in this book was correct at press time, the author and
publisher do not assume and hereby disclaim any liability to any party for
any loss, damage, or disruption caused by errors or omissions, whether such
errors or omissions result from negligence, accident, or any other cause.

Cover Image from My Life Graphic, ID: 141397459
Cover design by Michelle Manley of Graphique Designs, LLC
Book design and production by Jose Pepito and Redwood Publishing, LLC
Editing by Avery Auer
Sources cited on appropriate pages throughout

Contents

Dedication

I dedicate this book to the FastForward.ai team, which includes my co-founder, Romeo Ganescu, and every team member who has endeavored tirelessly, through COVID-19 and all the traditional start-up challenges, to make actionable the vision behind the new Social Retail Marketing paradigm of the Impatience Economy.

Acknowledgments

I spent the year of COVID-19 lockdowns at home, not traveling every week for the first time since college. I was focused on my new start-up and writing this book. So, despite the privilege of being at home, I was consumed with work. As always, my wife and family supported me through my craziness. I thank them eternally for that.

I also had the great support of my FastForward.ai team encouraging me, believing in me, and teaching me. Thank you!

And without God by my side, guiding my every step toward the goals and objectives ahead, I would never have advanced in anything, including writing and finishing this book.

Invitation: This Is the Future of Marketing

W HILE SCROLLING THROUGH INSTAGRAM, YOU TAG three friends under a video for Tim McGraw's new *Here on Earth* album. Your friends comment that the video was great. Suddenly, a notification pops up on your phone. You're not sure who it's from, but you're glad to receive it because you've just learned McGraw will be appearing in your city next month for a one-night-only concert. If you click, you can buy four tickets—in the third row.

You click, and somehow, you're moved into Facebook Messenger. You send a quick message to see if your friends would like to go. They respond with a fast and enthusiastic "Yes!" So you hurriedly click on the link inside your chat stream. Since your payment information is already stored in your Facebook settings, the transaction is complete in mere seconds.

You're going to the show.

As you and your friends start chatting about how excited you are to see McGraw (and maybe go out to eat before the show), you get another message. Again, you're not sure who sent it, and, still, you don't mind the intrusion. The offer: 20 percent off on a limo ride to the concert, complete with VIP entrance access.

How can you say no?

Now you're on a roll. From your prior searches, the channel knows you love northern Italian cuisine. It just so happens there's a fantastic new restaurant, featuring a hot Milanese chef, about eight blocks from the concert venue. Getting a reservation on a Saturday night? That will be impossible. But it seems that fortune suddenly favors you, and there is an available corner table with a view of the open kitchen—and a 15 percent discount on your dinner tab.

Just click here.

In a flash, you've got the whole night planned: the amazing concert tickets, the limo, and the dinner at a celebrated new restaurant. A few days before the show, as you feel your excitement building, you get an offer to send flowers on the day of the show. It's a great deal, and at 25 percent off, you accept and send a beautiful bouquet to a particularly special friend who will be coming along. But you invited three friends, how did "they" know you'd want to send flowers to one of them? Or *did* they? Was it a just a robotically generated offer? Who cares? You're happy they thought of it.

Not that many years ago, you might have considered this instant electronic monitoring of your intimate conversation to be an unwanted or outrageous intrusion. But today, you've made the compromise that we all have made: giving up part of your privacy in exchange for a sense of connection to a "super mind" that can practically predict your desires, even before you can mention them.

And, even better, gratify them quickly and easily.

You, my friend, are a citizen of the Age of Impatience™, a contented member of the Impatience Economy™. Two-day delivery? Are you kidding? Who could possibly wait that long? You want it *now*, and you get it *now*. Impatience drives the market, and the market satisfies the need to get everything you want *immediately and seamlessly.*

What about Amazon? They don't seem to be involved here. Isn't it the biggest store in the world right now? In fact, Amazon pales in comparison to the market The Impatience Economy is about to create. Around the world, approximately 200 *million* people belong to Amazon Prime. But within a few short years, *billions* will be buying everything from baby gifts to funeral arrangements the same way I described buying concert tickets, above: instantly, conveniently, and without friction.

This is a book about the dawn of the Second Consumer Revolution™ (I'll explain more about the First Consumer Revolution in Chapter 1). Driving this change is what I call The Impatience Economy. I'll describe how and why you and your company can and must participate in this new economy—or risk being left behind forever.

And of all things, the experience that kicked The Impatience Economy into high gear was none other than the COVID-19 pandemic.

In a matter of weeks, the pandemic jump-started an economic trend that will resonate for the entire twenty-first century. It isn't merely a new and slightly different normal; it's a new *abnormal,* at least compared to what's gone before. They say old habits die hard. Not anymore. Thanks to the COVID-19 pandemic lockdowns, old habits are changing on the spot. Everyone is affected—from age seven to seventy. Almost overnight, everything has become virtual and digital. Children attend Zoom classrooms and seniors conduct their Bible studies online. Adults work and shop from home. Social media is flourishing.

In addition to those who tragically lost their health or their lives during the pandemic, many companies will perish in the aftermath, unable to keep up with rapidly evolving consumer demands. What do those shoppers want? Everything. When do they want it? Right now. To sum up what Carrie Fisher wrote in *Postcards from the Edge:*The problem with immediate gratification is that it takes too long. That's where we are today—delayed gratification is no longer gratifying; it's become a contradiction in terms. Consumers want everything now, and they want it delivered to their door immediately.

Buy it now? Not good enough. *Get* it now—that's the real

desire. This book will show you how to capture and create new consumer segments and meet the faster and faster—seemingly impossible to satisfy—consumer demand to have everything, immediately.

Years ago, American Express ran an iconic ad campaign whose tagline was "Don't leave home without it." Today's consumers want the option of never leaving home. Period. And with Social Retail Marketing™ (SRM™), they don't have to. They don't even have to leave their social chat streams. The pandemic placed a huge premium on safety, as well as speed. People felt uncomfortable going to stores—even on the rare occasions when they were open. Consumers' buying habits shifted, and that shift has been made permanent. Those companies capable of responding to consumers' mounting impatience will be the big winners. Everyone else? They're headed for the dustbin of marketing and retail history.

Until now, consumers have had their choices made for them by the companies that could afford to spend the most money advertising their products through mass media. Whether you sold beer, insurance, cars, or candy, the bigger your marketing budget, the bigger your market share.

That's so 2018.

Today, consumers are no longer at the mercy of those with the biggest ad budgets. Instead, buyers now dictate what they want and how they want to receive, experience, and pay for those goods and services. Satisfying these consumers and mastering The Impatience Economy are not tasks for the fainthearted. The new terms are Darwinian. Not everyone will thrive—or survive. Successful companies must change their mindset, develop new skills, and adopt creative ways of thinking about technology, marketing, and retail channels. All others should begin preparing for new careers.

So, if you want to get under the hood of The Impatience Economy, if you want to understand this accelerating Age of

Impatience, pull up a chair. Having been the American founder and chairman emeritus of one of the world's largest telecom companies, having helped lead that company from zero to over 220 million customers—with a market cap on the NYSE of over $40 billion—I've learned a lot about meeting consumer needs, marketing, selling, and predicting where the world is going.

And I can tell you this with perfect confidence: the world is rapidly moving to a digital marketing and sales model at a speed unlike anything in human history.

If the COVID-19 pandemic lockdowns were the accelerant for The Impatience Economy, this book is the road map that shows executives and marketers how to succeed in the brave new world that has emerged. Combine the new consumer attitude toward speed, efficiency, and choice with the unbridled and, for the most part, untapped marketing power of social media platforms—those like Snapchat and Facebook, and others yet to be invented—and there's a whole new consumer universe to be understood, explored, and served.

A universe built on, of all things, impatience. In these pages, I'll show you how to get on board. We've no time to waste. Let's get started.

CHAPTER ONE

The Second Consumer Revolution™ Has Begun: Context and Catalyst

Hear The Rally Cry!

IN *FREE TO CHOOSE*, NOBEL PRIZE–WINNING ECONOMIST Milton Friedman says that enlightened societies enable consumers to pursue their own self-interests, buying the specific goods they want at the cheapest prices they can find. Today, both the degree of our freedom and the seamless precision of our choices are undergoing revolutionary changes. I'm referring here not just to the variety of available goods and services, but also to the speed with which they can be marketed, purchased, and delivered. For businesses that adapt to these changes and respond to emerging consumer demands, the coming years offer opportunities for unprecedented growth. Those who fail to heed this rallying cry and instead cling to the old models are doomed to the same fate as the rotting wooden hulks that ushered in an earlier age of innovation and mass consumerism.

The First Consumer Revolution

Before there was next-day Amazon delivery, there was the *East Indiaman*, the nickname given to any merchant ship belonging to the Dutch and British East India companies. Together, they dominated global trade from the seventeenth century to the nineteenth century. Their vast fleets ferried goods and raw materials between Asia, Africa, Europe, and the Americas. This expansive network of exchange helped give rise to the First Consumer Revolution.

Prior to the seventeenth century, being a *consumer* was a relatively unknown concept. Few citizens beyond monarchs, nobles, and wealthy merchants had the resources to spend on anything other than a narrow range of bare necessities: food, clothing, furniture, and household items. The first signs of a consumer age emerged in England near the end of the sixteenth century, when Queen Elizabeth—facing political pressure at home—increasingly demanded the English nobility maintain a more regular, active presence in the royal court. Inspired by the lavishness of the Italian example, she wanted the aristocrats in her orbit to demonstrate the same kind of opulence and flash.

Thus, nobles who wanted to earn the queen's attention and exert influence in the palace had to outdo one another. *Goods* became the currency of political jockeying; whoever could flaunt their finery and fashion most opulently asserted their status in the eyes of England's number one "influencer," the queen herself. This dynamic encouraged a spate of conspicuous consumption among the nobles who were competing for her attention.[1]

It also hinted at a broader change, one that would remake Western civilization and set the stage for the consumer ages to follow: the focus on *individual* rather than *collective* identity. The nobles looking to curry favor with the monarchy would have

---

[1] Grant McCracken, Culture and Consumption: New Approaches to the Symbolic Character of Consumer Goods and Activities, Bloomington: Indiana University Press, 1982

felt right at home in our age, when everyone has accepted the self-expressive nature of consumption—the notion that *what one buys shapes who one is.* Though this Elizabethan era trend was confined to a small coterie of elites, it planted the seeds of a consumerist revolution that would influence all strata of society in the centuries to come.

The Age of Discovery reached its peak in the seventeenth century. European powers traversed the globe, founding far-flung colonies, creating a network of new markets and trade routes, and establishing a global system of mercantile commerce. Although mercantilism remained the prevailing economic system, modern capitalism was emerging. Within the next two centuries, consumerism and capitalism would be joined in a happy marriage that endures to this day—the foundation of our modern economy.

By the start of the eighteenth century, the modern world had begun to take shape. The fledgling colonies of the New World had found their footing and become thriving trade centers, while back in Europe, London and Amsterdam had grown into economic powerhouses—the prosperous capitals of their respective nations' sprawling empires. Ultimately, this was a time of *discovery,* one in which consumers began to demand goods and services they did not previously know existed. This consumerism drove economic and social development, setting the stage for our contemporary global economy.

Dramatic changes occurred as we moved through periods of large-scale industrialization to the early stages of our own high-tech culture. The free flow of goods combined with greater purchasing power fueled the growing appetites of consumers for an ever-expanding range of products. But the increasing sophistication of those products should not obscure a century-spanning limitation: whether looking from a horse-drawn carriage at exotic fruits in a Paris market, staring through the coal-blackened window of a London spice shop, thumbing through a Sears catalog for a pair of bell-bottoms, or searching on the web for a discount bicycle, consumers have had relatively little control over the what, when, where, and how they obtained the goods they wanted. Producers and retailers set the rules, the shops, and the products offered, and consumers came to them. They followed the system.

That's about to change. Although many players in the digital consumer ecosystem can't see it yet, we've entered an amazing period of development and opportunity. It will be led by consumers' demands and desires, and supercharged by the synergistic power of 5G mobile, artificial intelligence, machine learning, virtual reality, and a distribution channel created by social media. Imagine the power of connecting 5.5 billion mobile users with instant, contextualized services that help shape their experiences and meet their desires. This is the extraordinary promise of what I'm calling the Second Consumer Revolution.

From Evolution to Revolution

Technology has always been a stepping stone for progress: sometimes evolutionary, sometimes revolutionary. *Evolutionary change,* such as we have witnessed throughout the First Customer Revolution, refers to steady, step-by-step innovation that occurs across an existing industry vertical. *Revolutionary change* occurs when innovation cuts across entire industries, bringing new value to consumers in ways they've never before experienced or imagined.

A simple analogy will make this distinction vivid and clarify the stakes for those hoping to thrive in the modern marketplace. Consider our primitive ancestors hunting saber-toothed tigers or defending their village with crude stone clubs. Over time, evolutionary technological change led them to identify flint as an especially promising raw material from which they could fashion progressively more and more lethally shaped spears and arrowheads with progressively more and more sophisticated stone-carving techniques. Each advance offered the inventive tribe a competitive advantage in obtaining food and fighting wars. It eventually established a lively munitions trade with nearby clans. For centuries, time spent refining those tools offered a substantial return on investment.

And then a revolutionary change occurred: a clever neighboring tribe invented gunpowder and metallurgy. Time-honored methods and accumulated wisdom suddenly accounted for nothing. Ongoing efforts to refine the old technology were delusional. The old tribe had a simple choice: adapt to the change or prepare for extinction. As we enter The Impatience Economy, the choice for businesses is equally stark: innovate or die.

The COVID-19 Effect On the Second Consumer Revolution

At the heart of the new revolution is a change in customer expectations. Apart from the staggering variety of products available to anyone with a credit card and an internet connection, what is most striking about the Second Consumer Revolution is the *speed* of the exchange. No longer must we wait for ships to cross the ocean or railroads to traverse the plains or the postman to drop off the package. Instant access, instant discovery, twenty-four-hour online shopping, delivery within an hour or two (or sooner), personalized algorithmic marketing—and everything bigger, better, and faster. Especially faster.

Internet speed and connectivity have accelerated at a breakneck pace and will work synergistically with social media, which is increasingly consumed on smartphones rather than personal computers. The telecom industry will invest nearly $1 trillion in 5G infrastructure over the next five years, enabling new business models and efficiencies in a wide range of verticals and services: retail, education, entertainment, finance, medicine, and government.

These trends were already reshaping the economic map

before 2020, but the COVID-19 pandemic catapulted us straight into a new era. Within a matter of weeks, the pandemic reordered the patterns of daily life worldwide; it was the spark that ignited a combustible set of elements already in place. We are living through the resulting explosion, which will incinerate the old and give rise to a revolutionary economic and business paradigm that will forever alter the way we do business and interact socially.

By forcing shops, schools, libraries, office buildings, movie theaters, stadiums, restaurants, and virtually all "nonessential" centers of public life to close, the pandemic drove most of the day-to-day activity we all took for granted out of the real world and onto the internet. Lockdowns compelled society to use digital, virtual, and social media in unprecedented ways. And not just e-commerce, which has surged since March 2020, but other activities we were accustomed to doing in conventional ways: how we learn, play, work, and eat have all gone online.

What's revolutionary about the development is that when COVID-19 struck, *everyone* had to get on board, and as fast as possible. Prior to the pandemic, social media remained the primary domain of the younger generations, especially the digital natives who grew up surfing, swiping, and scrolling. Suddenly, other demographics joined in. People in their fifties, sixties, and seventies, who may have had scant experience with video conferencing or ordering online products before the pandemic, now relied on these technologies to conduct business, communicate with family members, visit the doctor, and do their grocery shopping.

These digital newcomers included influential business owners, executives, and other prominent figures in the private sector. Many had been indifferent to social media. Now they were forced to engage with it. And as heads of important enterprises, they had to leverage these technologies to connect with consumers or watch the world pass them by.

Each week I talk to executives who had never used Zoom before and are now spending hours each day on the app. While something is certainly lost by the shift from in-person dialog to pixelated chats, new potentialities also arose. Again and again, people tell me they're able to talk with key contacts much more frequently and in greater depth now that travel time is no longer an issue.

This is not just a new method; it's a new mindset.

I had been predicting these developments for a long time. I could see that the elements for a new consumer paradigm were in place; all that was needed was the catalyst. I did not know what that would be. Then the coronavirus came, and changes that might have taken years happened almost overnight.

In the three months of the extreme COVID-19 lock-downs, e-commerce penetration growth matched that of the previous ten years, growing from 5.6 percent in 2009 to 16 percent in 2019 to 33 percent in April of 2020.

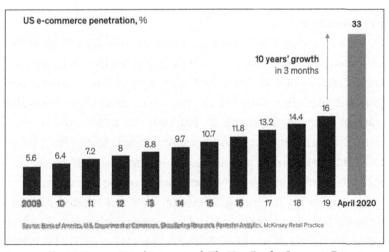

Periscope® by McKinsey, *Retail Reimagined: The New Era for Customer Experience,* August 2020

The virus itself will (we can presume) eventually go away. But its impact is here to stay. If you're an entrepreneur or a marketer, you can either adapt, or fall behind. There is no other option. Time's arrow flies in only one direction: forward.

Consumers in Control

Traditional marketing channels, distribution networks, and payment systems can no longer deliver what post-pandemic consumers want. They're tired of accepting a narrow range of choices or allowing themselves to be jerked around like puppets on a string. They don't want to sort through multiple app offerings or spend hours hunting for bargains. They don't want to drive to a store or walk through a mall. Their expectations are here and now, simple and easy, frictionless and personalized.

The old rules of traditional Marketing 101 no longer apply. Gone are the days when you could produce a generic magazine ad for a faceless Jane Doe and then wait for her to come to your retail store. Trust me—she's not coming. And she won't be visiting your website either.

To succeed in The Impatience Economy, you have to go to the customer, establish social media connections, understand her needs and interests, cultivate trust, and offer curated information about products that align with her desires. That information takes the place of your old, annoying ad, but with this difference: she now wants to hear from you. And because you're tracking her preferences and using artificial intelligence to anticipate her needs, you may ultimately come to know her better than she knows herself.

You're not a hectoring salesman. You're a trusted ally, informing her about products and experiences that are essential to the story line of her life. That's the advantage of Social Retail Marketing. And if she's a typical phone and social media user, you have the ability to connect with her for about three hours every day. So, let's say you know she admires a particular designer, and he's just come out with a new line of skirts. She's busy with work and counts on you to keep her updated on these developments. So you send her a photo. Maybe she buys the skirt; maybe she doesn't. Either way, you record the engagement so that your subsequent recommendations can be more precise. Soon you'll be using virtual reality to let her try on the skirts and see how they fit as she walks around her living room. And if she agonizes over whether to spend her vacation in Jakarta or Mexico City, you can let her take a virtual stroll around both cities until she makes up her mind.

With Social Retail Marketing, market research and product testing will occur automatically. You are already able to monitor in real time the response to various offers you display on social media, measuring people's engagement and purchase patterns. You can instantaneously use that data to make modifications in myriad ways: How do shoppers react if you change the color from black to blue? Or offer Model AB30 instead of AB29? Or package one item with something else in the catalog?

With real-time, digitized, automated feedback, you no longer need to rely on experts to judge or focus group data to extrapolate through models until you understand what people want. You can vacuum up all that data straight from the source, in real time, using advanced analytics and AI technology to A/B test—second by second—precisely what people prefer.

> *If data is the new oil, then insights from that data are the new renewable energy. And therein lies the real promise.*

> Renewable energy—actionable insights and cutting-edge analytics—is the future. I'll discuss this topic in more detail later in this book.

These changes demonstrate how, in The Impatience Economy, individual consumer desires have become untethered from the top-down tyranny of the tastemakers. Consumers demonstrate through their preferences and actions what they want. The consumer market has been fragmented into a million pieces, as each person can retreat to his own specialized, curated corner and seek out products that conform to his tastes. Each individual has become a target demographic unto himself.

Production has followed this trend. Take a few minutes to peruse the web, and you'll see that there's a product and service for virtually every conceivable consumer desire, no matter how obscure—although we've barely scratched the surface of how social media can be adapted to fulfill those wishes. And not just to fulfill them, but also to anticipate them—to give the online consumer what she wants before she even knows she wants it. As Steve Jobs famously stated, "Our job is to figure out what they're going to want before they do. . . . People don't know what they want until you show it to them."

As we will see in the next chapter, even Amazon, with its dominance of e-commerce and its dizzying array of products, will soon look inadequate compared to what Social Retail Marketing can offer. That inadequacy will become even more pronounced as socially driven retail and marketing expands into new channels and uses even more granular, algorithmically fine-tuned product offerings than what Amazon has achieved with its massive data operation. Amazon may be an economic juggernaut, but its total of 197 million monthly visitors[2] looks puny compared to the 3.8 billion users of social media worldwide[3]—an incomprehensibly vast market that we haven't had the means or the technology to fully tap. Until now.

---

[2] Emily Dayton, "Amazon Statistics You Should Know: Opportunities to Make the Most of America's Top Online Marketplace," BigCommerce.com, https://www.bigcommerce.com/blog/amazon-statistics/

[3] Simon Kemp, "Digital 2020: 3.8 Billion People Use Social Media," WeAreSocial.com, Jan. 30, 2020, https://wearesocial.com/blog/2020/01/digital-2020-3-8-billion-people-use-social-media

Tremendous opportunities for productivity are opening up in ways that few of us have ever imagined. The consumer desires convenience, lifestyle, peace of mind, and freedom—freedom from regulation and freedom to choose what, when, where, and how to consume.

And what else does the consumer want? Everything.

When? A minute ago.

Welcome to The Impatience Economy.

As 5G mobile, AI, social media, advanced analytics, and other technologies come together to create a new paradigm, the benefits will be enormous. Producers and marketers will have novel ways of getting their products into the hands of people who want them, and consumers will have more choice and convenience than ever. Enterprises will thrive. Nations will prosper.

But this is not a recipe for utopianism. As always, new opportunities bring new challenges and new risks. We must not ignore concerns about privacy. We must keep in mind that technology is morally neutral: it can be used for good or ill. It can be leveraged to liberate or to control and manipulate. Consumers will have more freedom, but freedom can be abused. And sometimes, giving people exactly what they want is perilous, if what they want happens to be destructive to them and to society at large. These are important questions we must answer as we adapt to a revolutionary era.

The changes are irreversibly in motion, but the situation remains fluid. We can't put the genie back in the bottle (nor would we want to), but we can choose carefully the wishes we ask him to grant. We live in exciting times. An old order is falling away, and a new one is taking its place. That is scary, exhilarating, confusing, challenging, and edifying all at once.

But above all, for business leaders, it is an opportunity that must not be squandered.

In the next chapter I'll substantiate how the Second Consumer Revolution has given rise to The Impatience Economy, and how Social Retail Marketing will grow to be bigger than Amazon. Really!

CHAPTER TWO

Why Social Retail Marketing™ (SRM™) Will Be Bigger Than Amazon

Are You Crazy?

WHENEVER I SAY THAT SOCIAL RETAIL MARKETING will be bigger than Amazon, people look at me with the same troubled expressions Aristotle identified on the faces of those watching the plays of Sophocles, Euripides, Aeschylus, and the other authors of Greek tragedy: fear and pity. Like the protagonists in those plays, I'm seen as someone in the grip of a profound mind-deranging flaw. Like a man infected by rabies, I'm not only beyond the help of humane intervention, but I'm a threat to the sanity of everyone in my perimeter. Reasoning with me is both futile and dangerous. Best to give me a wide berth, and hope I bite someone else.

After all, in 2016, 64 percent of American households subscribed to Amazon Prime, 9 percent more than voted in that year's presidential election and 13 percent more than attended church on a regular basis.[4] In 2019, the average small and medium-sized enterprises (SME) sold more than four thousand items per minute on the platform, more than 2.5 million sellers used the Amazon marketplace, and the company brought in more than $75.5 billion in sales revenue during the first quarter of 2020.[5] With a business model that specifies (a bit grandiosely), "Our goal is to be earth's most customer-centric company,"[6] Amazon seems to be an unassailable Goliath. Who in his right mind could possibly champion an unassuming, unheralded David—armed with a sling and a few pebbles—against this battle-tested titan?

Of course, the boyish David proved himself the better man. A careful observer might have predicted this outcome—might have recognized that the Hebrew shepherd's fighting strategy—honed against lions and bears—would serve him well against a lumbering Philistine giant. A similarly careful assessment of the current marketplace will reveal that my predictions about SRM are grounded in facts, not hyperbole—in realistic assessments of the current market, not awestruck and defeatist acceptance of the status quo. And while I don't want to overextend my battle metaphor (Amazon, unlike Goliath, is not going to collapse and die), the greater potential of SRM looks obvious as soon as one turns to the numbers—especially as they relate to the breadth of the market.

Amazon's achievements are impressive. In January 2020, *Fortune* reported that the company had more than 156 million Prime users worldwide.[7] But as the table below reveals, the three

---

[4] Scott Galloway, *The Four: The Hidden DNA of Amazon. Apple, Facebook, and Google* (New York: Penguin Random House, 2018)

[5] Maryam Mohsin, *10 Amazon Statistics You Need to Know in 2020*, https://www.oberlo.com/blog/amazon-statistics

[6] Brad Stone, *The Everything Store: Jeff Bezos and the Age of Amazon* (New York: Back Bay Books, 2014)

[7] Don Reisinger, "Amazon Prime's numbers (and influence) continue to grow," *Fortune*, January 16, 2020

most popular social media networks each had at least two *billion* users, all potential SRM consumers. Our brains have not evolved to distinguish differences on this scale with much precision, so take a moment to consider the following:

- A million seconds is twelve days.
- A billion seconds is thirty-one years.

Keep that distinction in mind as you compare Amazon Prime users to social media users. Does my assertion that SRM will be bigger than Amazon still seem the delusional product of a rabid brain? Note that Facebook has 2.6 billion users, WhatsApp has two billion users, and even the sixteenth-ranked social media network (i.e., Twitter) has twice as many users as Amazon Prime. Still want to bet on Goliath?

Most Popular Social Media Networks Worldwide (January 2021)	
Network	*Users (billions)*
Facebook	2.740
YouTube	2.291
WhatsApp	2.000
Facebook Messenger	1.300
Instagram	1.221
Weixin/WeChat	1.213
TikTok	0.689
QQ	0.617
Douyin	0.600
Sina Weibo	0.511
Telegram	0.500
Snapchat	0.498
Kuaishou	0.481

Pinterest	0.442
Reddit	0.430
Twitter	0.353
Quora	0.300

Source: *https://www.statista.com/statistics/272014/global-social-networks-ranked-by-number-of-users/*

Convenience Counts

In addition to the vast difference in potential customers, consider the matter of convenience. Most people ask, "What could be easier than Amazon?" The answer is SRM, which is Amazon without the app. To buy something on Amazon requires three steps: open the app, search for the product, and buy it. My vision for SRM is much more direct. Say you're watching a video on YouTube, and you see a guy wearing a leather jacket. It looks good. You want it. In an optimized SRM experience, you simply click on the jacket, and two hours later, it's at your house, in your size. You're wearing it as you go out to dinner.

So "What could be easier than Amazon?" is no longer a rhetorical question—because what I've just described is easier than Amazon.

Now, you may think the difference is trivial. But I maintain it is not. Not in The Impatience Economy. This is an age in which a product named Slydial allows you to suppress the recipient's ringtone when you return phone calls, so your call goes directly to voicemail, where you can avoid time-wasting conversations and leave a message expressing your regrets for not connecting with the person you've just taken elaborate pains to avoid. This is an age when, if you don't have time to read a book, you can listen to it on Audible at up to 3.5 times the speed of the original recording. And if even that verbal torrent is too slow, you can use a product such as Blinkist to give you a fifteen-minute summary of Thomas

Piketty's dauntingly nuanced 816-page *Capital in the Twenty-First Century* or Max Tegmark's equation-laden, innumeracy-exposing *Our Mathematical Universe: My Quest for the Ultimate Nature of Reality,* so you can impress your friends at the next cocktail party, assuming, of course, that you don't consider such gatherings a waste of time.

Given the demand for these kinds of time-sparing products, why wouldn't we expect users to be deterred by the added step of having to work through an app? Why wouldn't they prefer a direct, less annoying, more time-efficient approach? Why wouldn't they prefer to click on the shirt Brad Pitt is sporting in their social media feed, and have it delivered before the video ends? And recent trends show that this is precisely what they do prefer. Consumers are sick of cluttering up their mobile screens with app icons from every store in the world. As a result, app download rates are now expressed as negative numbers. People are taking them off their phones. And the approach I'm advocating enables them to continue doing so. How? By moving the retail and marketing channel inside a social media stream. Think about it. No one spends hours and hours each day in the Amazon app. But that's exactly what billions of consumers do with Facebook, YouTube, Instagram, and other social media networks.

Don't misunderstand me: Amazon is awesome. As Brad Stone says in his excellent analysis of the company's history, it's "the everything store." But the word *store* is telling here. In Chapter 1, I made the point that we've entered a new paradigm, one in which the company has to go to the customer rather than the other way around. And Amazon hasn't really done that. It's changed the brick-and-mortar retail experience, but the onus is still on customers to download the app or go to the website, and search for what they want. They still need to go to Amazon. It's not coming to them. To me, that falls far short of their goal of being the world's most customer-centric company. And that failure provides an opportunity for producers and marketers who adopt the SRM approach. It's not fully up and running yet. Amazon still has an outsized impact. But the Second Consumer Revolution and The Impatience Economy are already changing the ground rules.

The Medium Is the Message

According to J. Clement at Statista.com, e-commerce—as a share of total US retail sales—has more than doubled over the last seven years, from less than 6 percent in 2013 to 12.4 percent in 2020. You don't need to be Nostradamus to see that online purchases are going to outpace brick-and-mortar purchases in the years to come. People just don't want to go to a store. So there's an enormous growth potential here. And who's going to reap those profits? Anyone with the foresight to get inside the SRM channel and establish a trusted relationship with customers. For those media-savvy businesses, the money is there for the taking.

In his 1964 book *Understanding Media: The Extensions of Man,* Marshall McLuhan coined an enigmatic phrase that entered the popular imagination, where it resonates with even greater force in our internet age than it did when the book appeared: "the medium is the message."[8] I'm simplifying a bit, but McLuhan's main point was that the means by which a message is transmitted (e.g., smoke signals, speech, print, radio, television) matters almost as much as the content itself.

This is precisely my point in discussing the social media medium. One can deliver the same general information about a pair of shoes in various formats: on a billboard or in a magazine ad, a TV commercial, or a social media feed. But if the aim of your message is to sell the shoes, the medium matters. And SRM is far and away the most likely means of achieving that aim, in large part because you're putting consumers first, you're freeing them from outside control over what, when, where, and how they consume.

[8] Marshall McLuhan, *Understanding Media: The Extensions of Man* (Cambridge, Massachusetts: MIT Press, 1964)

Keep in mind that information flows in both directions across the SRM channels. That opens up a whole new era of product placement. In the old model, businesses had to survey consumers, make educated guesses about where the market was headed, develop products based on those guesses, and then invest millions of dollars trying to shape buying trends and drive sales toward products they'd already made. That's a high-risk way to work because if your crystal ball is a tad cloudy, you're stuck with a warehouse full of inventory nobody wants. In the new model, you simply monitor the social media feeds to see what people want, and you make products and services based on that data. You're no longer trying to create the trend. You're just reading it from the data and using artificial intelligence to help interpret that data so that you can take advantage of the trend and actually even amplify a trend. You don't have to hope and pray your strategy works, because the consumer has already shaped the strategy.

And it costs very little. You pay Google, a small amount to Instagram, a little to Facebook, a little to TikTok. But all of this is just a fraction of your old marketing budget. Social Retail Marketing upends the traditional advertising and marketing industries because you no longer need to spend a fortune on ads. Instead, you can get more reliable information on social media while saving money. And that will be crucial to small businesses and to the so-called mom-and-pop shops. They no longer need to make a Faustian bargain with Amazon on the marketing and sales side. That's huge. That levels the playing field, increases competition, reduces prices, and forms another key component of The Impatience Economy. Suddenly, a big power like Amazon is going to have a thousand—or maybe ten thousand—competitors for every product it sells. And unless it stays nimble, it's going to suffer.

The old joke was that half the money spent on marketing was wasted, but we just didn't know which half. In reality, the ratio was not 50:50. It was more like 99 percent wasted to 1 percent effective. Now, though, you can spend just the 1 percent, keep the rest, and see exactly what happens with those funds because you can track them. You're like a nearsighted child who puts on a pair of glasses for the first time: what has been hazy suddenly becomes clear. It's as though for years you've been betting on horse races, studying the matchups, monitoring the weather, reading tarot cards, comparing horses' horoscopes, losing thousands of dollars every few weeks, and then you find a bookie who lets you place a bet as the jockeys ride the last turn of the last lap. For the first time in your life, you understand the meaning of "a sure thing." You're never going back to the old system again.

Facing the Revolution

Any period of rapid technological change provokes a wide range of hopes and fears. My view is one of robust optimism. I see consumers living freer, more prosperous, and happier lives as businesses use personal data from SRM channels to provide carefully curated goods and services. I see consumers willingly providing that data in the hope of discovering products and services they didn't know exist. Finally, I think the Second Consumer Revolution and Social Retail Marketing will move us beyond the narrow Amazon model and generate benefits at every level of society, from the individual to the collective.

But I'm mindful that not everyone shares my optimism. Perhaps the least optimistic voice belongs to the well-known author and computer scientist Jaron Lanier, one of the founders of virtual reality. He sees "social networking sites as . . . a method of violating privacy and dignity"[9] and asks, "How can you remain autonomous in a world where you are under constant surveillance and are constantly prodded by algorithms run by some of the richest corporations in history, which have

---

[9] Jaron Lanier, *You Are Not a Gadget: A Manifesto* (New York: Vintage Books, 2011)

no way of making money except by being paid to manipulate your behavior?"[10]

Israeli historian Yuval Noah Harari takes a much less strident position. Though he is wryly grateful that Amazon's algorithm "knows me" and offers him book recommendations, an ominous undercurrent colors his tone:

> Devices such as Amazon's Kindle are able to collect data on their users while they are reading the book. For example, your Kindle can monitor which parts of the book you read fast, and which slow; on which page you took a break, and on which sentence you abandoned the book, never to pick it up again. . . . If Kindle is upgraded with face recognition and biometric sensors, it can know what made you laugh, what made you sad, and what made you angry. Soon, books will read you while you are reading them. And whereas you quickly forget most of what you read, Amazon will never forget a thing. Such data will enable Amazon to evaluate the suitability of a book much better than ever before. It will also enable Amazon to know exactly who you are and how to turn you on and off.[11]

To differing degrees, both writers express a lack of trust in the purveyors of technology. Lanier sees an Orwellian nightmare straight out of *1984*. Harari's vision is closer to Huxley's *Brave New World*, in which we quietly and comfortably participate in the surrender of our autonomy. Well-informed cautionary voices

---

[10] Jaron Lanier, *Ten Arguments for Deleting Your Social Media Accounts Right Now* (New York: Henry Holt and Company, 2019)
[11] Yuval Noah Harari, *Homo Deus: A Brief History of Tomorrow* (London: Harvill Secker, Vintage Books, 2016)

are always worth considering, especially when they address complex issues about which decent people can disagree. But I would submit that both writers are overreacting. They mistake a mutually beneficial relationship for a zero-sum game. In their attempts to protect us from exaggerated risks, they misunderstand the essence of the Second Consumer Revolution in ways that may—through an excess of caution—prevent them and others from enjoying its benefits.

Below are five steps businesses can take to reassure the naysayers and help fulfill my prediction that Social Retail Marketing will be bigger and better than Amazon.

1. Fulfill consumers' desires for convenience, lifestyle, peace of mind, and freedom.
2. Help consumers discover products and services they don't know exist.
3. Develop a two-way relationship that is not just about selling, but about building trust and relevance.
4. Offer consumers value and purpose, and they will happily allow you to harness their profiles and data.
5. Invest in new digital channels and technology so consumers can control what, where, when, and how they consume. Platforms like Fastforward.ai, Facebook Messenger, Instagram Checkout, and WhatsApp Business now offer opportunities to conduct commerce inside social media and messaging feeds. Focus on marketing, re-marketing, and building relationships through these channels.

In 2019, global e-commerce sales totaled $3.4 *trillion*, a mere 16 percent of all retail. That figure is projected to double by 2022. By way of comparison, Amazon's annual sales for the same period were $280 *billion*. To appreciate the magnitude of that difference, consider the following:

- A billion seconds is 31 years
- A trillion seconds is 31,688 years

Thirty-one years ago was 1990. George Herbert Walker Bush was the president. Thirty-one thousand years ago was the Stone Age. Keep that in mind as you reconsider your initial reaction to my claim that Social Retail Marketing will be bigger and better than Amazon.

Do you still think I'm crazy?

Do you still want to bet on Goliath?

Don't miss this opportunity. Do your part to lead the Second Consumer Revolution and succeed in The Impatience Economy. Take your share of the unstoppable growth.

In the next chapter, I'll explain why this is a truly revolutionary development and why it requires your immediate attention.

CHAPTER THREE

Digital Journeys

The Life You Had? That's Over!

"'M SORRY ABOUT WHAT HAPPENED TO YOU. BUT THE most important thing is, you understand the life you once had, *is gone.* The choice you have is about the life you have next."

This speech—perhaps the most moving in FX's 2020 artificial-intelligence series *Devs*—conveys an idea that many CEOs and marketing executives are hearing (or ought to be hearing) with the dawn of the Second Consumer Revolution. Lots of them have resisted. They've tried to believe that social media is just a lot of millennial nonsense, like cancel culture, trigger warnings, safe spaces, purple bangs, and participation trophies. The purpose of this chapter is to convince them that, with respect to SRM, they are wrong.

The character in *Devs* has to completely and instantly change the way she sees the world, or she is going to die. She has to recognize that everything she thought she knew about her life prior to this minute no longer has any relevance. The same is true for business leaders. Hanging on to the past, living with entrenched attitudes, trusting the status quo, sentimentalizing old triumphs, giving in to nostalgia—none of these are options. Revolutions are scary; not everyone survives. Change takes courage. If you can convince yourself there's a way out, you'll fail to summon that courage. Guaranteed. But the truth is that there is no way out. You're facing a binary choice: be brave or be finished.

The CEO's Journey: Upending the Old

In the pre-internet era, marketing was a monolithic, high-dollar, undemocratic industry. Businesses had three basic options: television, radio, and print. Fortune 500 companies traditionally spent billions developing slick TV commercials and paid to air them at the most widely watched events, such as the Super Bowl, the Masters Tournament, and the Emmys. They placed expensive ads in glossy trend-setting publications, such as *Vanity Fair, Vogue,* and *GQ.* Smaller companies had to settle for radio spots on the local stations, TV spots during college football games, ads on city billboards, or tacky inserts in newspapers.

The term *broadcasting* suggests the inherent limitations of this approach. Most of us forget (or never knew) that this word was in wide use centuries before the invention of radio waves. It described a quick, inefficient agricultural practice in which a farmer scattered seeds, often across unplowed earth, fully aware that only a small fraction of them would germinate. Like an oak tree dropping thousands of acorns, most of which will be eaten by squirrels or die in the sun-starved and infertile earth beneath the parent's canopy, the farmer hoped to offset the inefficiency of the process by the volume of the output.

The marketing broadcast is equally inefficient. The producer throws a generic message in the consumer's face on a one-way channel, interrupting the program everyone wants to watch, in the full knowledge that only a few members of the audience are potential buyers. During the 2020 Super Bowl, for example, Porsche spent $10.2 million for a sixty-second spot advertising the Taycan, its first fully electric car.[12] But how many viewers need a new car? And what fraction of those can afford a model with a starting price of $79,990? And how many of those were taking a bathroom break during the time-out when the ad aired so they didn't miss part of the game? How many used one of the myriad ad-blocking strategies available to consumers? Businesses that purchase TV commercials are the advertising equivalent of the stranded islander who corks a note in a bottle and tosses it into the sea. Moreover, the advertiser has no way of tracking the ad's impact on the few people with the money to buy the car, no way of determining whether another approach would have reached more potential buyers, or what parts of the message resonated—or failed to resonate—with the audience.

Perversely, the practice continues despite the knowledge that it isn't working. As Anthony Puntoriero notes, "Think about how disastrous it is for these Fortune 500 companies to invest millions upon millions of dollars on advertisements that do not yield a positive return on investment. If any at all."[13] Gary Vaynerchuk echoes this point:

> Every person here grabs [his or her phone] any time that there is a commercial. Yet $80 billion is spent by the biggest brands in the world to make thirty-second videos of a Jeep going up a hill, or some guy grabbing a beer, or some lady with a baby, using some oil. Eighty billion dollars! It's completely not practical. It is broken. And it's the

---

[12] Mark Matousek, "Porsche Bought Its First Super Bowl Ad in over 20 Years to Promote the Taycan," *Business Insider*, January 28, 2020

[13] Anthony Puntoriero, "Fortune 500 Companies Waste $80 Billion Each Year on TV Commercials," (*Medium*, September 21, 2018)

reason that 95 percent of the Fortune 500 biggest brands in the world have declined in market share over the last two years.[14]

At FastForward.ai, I emphasize to CEOs that their money could deliver a far more substantial return on investment if they embrace an SRM approach, if they abandon the familiar path and embark on a new journey. But far too many of them simply can't break with the status quo or override the objections of their hidebound marketing departments. So their companies end up like a promising young fighter under the misguided tutelage of an old-school trainer. They employ outdated workout and dietary regimens because they can't bring themselves to trust the latest science-based innovations. They crack a raw egg into a glass of beer and gulp it down because this is what (allegedly) worked for Sugar Ray Robinson or some champ from a bygone era. And even after they show up flat and overtrained and get mauled, they return to the gym and double down on the same strategy. It's sad. It's dumb. And at some level, though they don't like to hear this, it's cowardly. Because it's a refusal to face the truth.

I once watched a bird that had flown through the open door of a dark warehouse. He headed straight for the glass transom in the roof because he could see the sun and the sky beyond it. Again and again, he crashed into the glass and fell to the ground. There was nothing I could do for him. He literally battered himself to death because he couldn't accept that the "obvious" path to freedom was blocked. And he couldn't convince himself to resist his instinct and launch himself into the unknown and frightening darkness, which was his only route to survival. And I'm sorry to say it, but I think of that bird whenever I talk to CEOs imprisoned by their own outmoded ideas.

Joseph Chilton Pearce made a point that manages to be both

---

[14] Gary Vaynerchuk, "How to Waste $80 Billion" (https://www.youtube.com/watch?v=ZkTqAJrswJ0)

obvious and profound about leadership during revolutionary times: "You can't build a new foundation by digging the same hole deeper. *Vertical thinking* keeps excavating the same ruin. *Lateral thinking* looks for a new place to dig."[15] The courage to make that lateral leap is what will distinguish those who thrive in The Impatience Economy from those who die asserting that what worked in the past will work in the future.

The Wartime CEO

Imprisoned by Benito Mussolini, the Italian philosopher Antonio Gramsci aptly described periods of revolutionary change: "The crisis consists precisely in the fact that the old is dying and the new is struggling to be born; in this interregnum a great variety of morbid symptoms appear."[16] In the "interregnum" created the Second Consumer Revolution "morbid symptoms" abound. Leaving aside the commercial effects of the coronavirus pandemic, we see businesses struggling—and often failing—to adapt to new market conditions and consumer demands.

All the old practices and certainties are either failing or about to fail. Consider that only two of the top ten retailers in 1990 are still thriving today. Or that Macy's lost 80 percent of its value from April 2019 to April 2020. As the chart below suggests,[17] Gramsci's phrase *the old is dying* is mortally relevant to our age.

Ben Horowitz's distinction between peacetime and wartime CEOs highlights the kind of leadership required to abandon time-tested marketing formulas and boldly face the new realities. Like it or not, every business now needs a wartime CEO. As Horowitz says of his own experience in this role, "I follow the first principle

---

[15] Joseph Chilton Pearce, *The Crack in the Cosmic Egg: New Constructs of Mind and Reality* (New York: Simon and Schuster, 2002)

[16] Antonio Gramsci, *Prison Notebooks* (New York: Columbia University Press, 2011)

[17] Mawdud Chouchdry, "Brick and Mortar US Retailer Market Value: 2006 to 2016," *ExecTech*

of the Bushido—the way of the warrior: keep death in mind at all times." He emphasizes that the most important characteristic of such leaders is courage—particularly as it relates to resisting the status quo: "In my experience as CEO, I found that the most important decisions tested my courage far more than my intelligence. The right decision is often obvious, but the pressure to make the wrong decision can be overwhelming."[18]

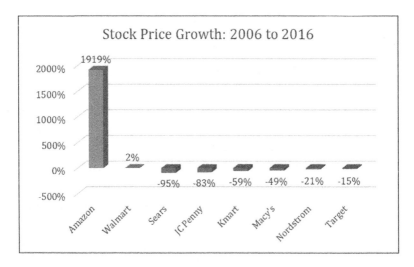

Stock Price Growth: 2006 to 2016

Transformational change that upends conventional wisdom can only come from a wartime CEO. It has to be driven from the top down. Midlevel employees have far too much investment in the status quo. To some extent, small organizations have an advantage here. They are nimbler. Think of the difference between turning over a kayak and turning over an aircraft carrier. It's just a matter of physics, the laws of inertia. In a big organization, you're going to have marketing people come in with their charts and graphs, and the CEO simply has to tell them, "Look I understand what you're recommending, but the thing is, we've been slipping

---

[18] Ben Horowitz, *The Hard Thing about Hard Things: Building a Business When There Are No Easy Answers* (New York: Harper Collins, 2014)

3 to 4 percent a year for the last fifteen years, and we've had to close sixty stores in the past year (or 125 if you're Macy's), so I'm overruling you. We're going to make this change. Period." A recent *New Yorker* cartoon perfectly captures this crucial moment of self-assertion: a resolute CEO is sitting at the head of a meeting table, looking at all his top employees, and with a stern expression declares, "What I'm proposing is this. *No.*" That's funny, but it takes a lot of guts to say, "We're making a change, and I may not fully understand it, and I know you disagree with me, but we're doing it anyway." It takes a wartime CEO.

"What I'm proposing is this. No."

Horowitz is great on this point, and every business leader should commit these epigrammatic points to memory:

- In peacetime, leaders must maximize and broaden the current opportunity. As a result, peacetime leaders employ techniques to encourage broad-based creativity and contribution across a broad set of possible objectives. In wartime, by contrast, the company typically has a single bullet in the chamber and must, at all costs, hit the target. The company's survival in wartime depends on strict adherence and alignment to the mission.

- Peacetime CEO knows that the proper protocol leads to winning. Wartime CEO violates protocol in order to win.
- Peacetime CEO always has a contingency plan. Wartime CEO knows sometimes you gotta roll a hard six.
- Peacetime CEO aims to *expand* the market. Wartime CEO aims to *win* the market.
- Peacetime CEO strives for broad-based buy-in. Wartime CEO neither indulges in consensus building nor tolerates disagreements.
- Peacetime CEO trains her employees to ensure satisfaction and career development. Wartime CEO trains her employees so they don't get their asses shot off in the battle.
- Peacetime CEO thinks of the competition as other ships in a big ocean that may never engage. Wartime CEO thinks the competition is sneaking into her house and trying to kidnap her children.
- Peacetime CEO has rules like "we're going to exit all businesses where we're not number one or number two." Wartime CEO often has no businesses that are number one or two and therefore does not have the luxury of following that rule.

The Consumers' Journey

If the first part of my challenge at FastForward.ai is to convince CEOs that their survival requires them to journey beyond conventional marketing practices, the second part is to teach them how necessary it is to create journeys for their customers and systematically evaluate those journeys to increase sales. On the most technical level, marketers use "journey" to describe the path a consumer takes before buying a product. Now, with traditional advertising, the touchpoints in that progression are impossible to track. There isn't any journey. You haven't created one. You run a TV ad during a Dallas Cowboys football game, and if your sales increase in the viewing area over the next week, you assume that the ad accounted for that increase. But this is a very crude measurement. You don't have any sense of who is (or isn't) responding to the ad or what parts are (or aren't) persuasive or whether a different kind of approach might have produced better (or worse) results. The same is true with something like a digital billboard in a Google ad or a Facebook ad. You're still essentially blind to the complex chain of events that leads to a purchase.

With SRM, however, all of that changes. Now, when you show people something—the image of a dress shirt, for example—you're establishing a two-way channel. You know precisely how many people clicked on it and what those people have in common. You can create multiple journeys and use simple A/B testing to determine if you get a greater response for a red shirt or a blue shirt, an indoor or outdoor setting, a handsome model or a regular-looking Joe, a famous person with blue eyes or a man on the street with brown eyes—or (to stick with our dress-shirt example) the Hathaway man. His swashbuckling eyepatch, which cost five cents at the time, created a million dollars in sales and moved the company from relative obscurity to its position as the second largest US shirtmaker.[19] Why? Because it told a story. An obscure, nondescript model became a man out of a Hemingway tale or a John le Carré spy novel. The company ran ads showing him playing the cello, holding a shotgun, standing at a blackboard in front of a complex set of physics equations. Consumers couldn't look at this this guy without lingering a moment, wondering who

---

[19] Alex Walker, "How a 5-Cent Eye-Patch Created a Million Dollar Story," *Sitepoint*, November 11, 2015 https://www.sitepoint.com/50-cent-eye-patch-created-million-dollar-story/

he was and how he'd gotten hurt and if the shirt might offer them the same air of mystery.

You get the idea. The point is to design journeys based on data you can track. You give consumers choices, see what they choose as they swipe or click from one box to another, and then you fine-tune the next iterations. You're setting up a Darwinian process in which the consumer exerts the selection pressure, and your messages adapt to the market environment. It's survival of the fittest. After each computerized assessment of the data—because you don't need people to do this—you're moving closer and closer to the marketing equivalent of Secretariat and further away from some generic, swaybacked nag giving kids two-dollar rides at a county fair. You can't do that with a static image in *People* magazine or a commercial you play over and over until people want to puncture their eardrums and gouge out their eyes. You can't build a relationship with the consumer that way. Nor can you do so by simply giving traditional single-direction ads a quick digital patina.

The average consumer is exposed to seventeen hundred banner ads each month, but fails to notice—let alone respond to—more than half of them.[20] Moreover, just "going digital" in an uninformed way can be counterproductive. Suppose you send out a blatant, heavy-handed ad, and you promise the recipients a discount if they share that ad with their friends, most of whom will be annoyed for being spammed. This isn't social media. It's *anti-social* media. Over time, you're more likely to lose customers than gain them.

As Tim Staples notes in *Break Through the Noise: The Nine Rules to Capture Global Attention*,[21] the single most important challenge for social retail marketers is to provide stories that consumers want to share:

---

[20] Goran Dautovic, "The 45 Most Important Advertising Statistics of 2020," *Smallbizgenius*, August 12, 2020

[21] Tim Staples and Josh Young, *Break through the Noise: The Nine Rules to Capture Global Attention* (New York: Houghton, Mifflin, Harcourt, 2019)

Being shareable means that you create content with such high value for the people viewing it that they are *compelled* to share it with their friends. This mindset puts the consumer first and builds a relationship *before* attempting to sell, essentially the opposite of traditional advertising's approach.

The share is the most coveted action. It commands the highest premium and delivers the most value. That's because a share is what turns your audience into your brand ambassador.

Word-of-mouth recommendations from friends have always been the most persuasive form of advertising. But they've never been scalable. Even if your ambassador was riding a Kawasaki Ninja crotch rocket while shouting through a bullhorn, his words were never going to reach many potential buyers.

But that was before social media. People who use Facebook, Instagram, Twitter, TikTok, YouTube, and other platforms are constantly sharing what they like with their friends or followers. You'll need to develop separate journeys and stories tailored to the specifics of each platform, but the payoffs for doing so are impossible to overstate. Consider this: if you send a message to fifty million Facebook users and 2 percent like it, you've just picked up a million ambassadors. You're now part of a million stories. And when your new ambassadors share your message with their friends, the number of journeys you've set in motion compounds, and then some fraction of that group shares it with their friends, and then some fraction of that group . . .

But even that is not the end of the good news—because by analyzing data on the likes and shares, you can start to form various profiles of others on Facebook who might respond positively to your message. And as Scott Galloway points out, "As measured by adoption and usage, Facebook is the most successful thing in the history of humankind." There are 7.5 billion people in the world, and Facebook has a meaningful relationship with 2.2 billion of them. Its social network registers fifty minutes of a typical user's day. One in six minutes spent online is with Facebook, and one in five minutes spent on mobile is with Facebook."[22] When I talk about the power of SRM, I'm not blowing smoke. I'm simply citing the facts.

Creating Sharable Stories: A Case Study

Because every business has to draw on its own history and products to develop a personal relationship with consumers, no one can offer a step-by-step rubric for you to follow. If you simply imitate a model, you're establishing an *impersonal* relationship. As Ben Horowitz says, I can't "provide a recipe for challenges that have no recipes. There's no recipe for really complicated, dynamic situations . . . . That's the hard thing about hard things—there is no formula for dealing with them." That said, I can provide an example that will clarify the essential dos and don'ts of SRM relationships in a way you can adapt to your own particulars.

A friend of mine works at SAS Institute, one of the largest privately held software companies in the world. Its primary focus and largest revenue stream is business analytics. A traditional marketing approach would be to offer testimonials from users or to present side-by-side comparisons with the products of rival companies. Our graphs are better than their graphs! But we know that modern consumers reject blatant attempts to scream, "Buy me!" Such stories begin and end with an (almost always unsuccessful) sales pitch. Think of it: a company offering infomercial-like details by computer geeks engaged in the spine-tingling process of analyzing data and telling you that (go figure), their product is

---

[22] Scott Galloway, *The Four: The Hidden DNA of Amazon, Apple, Facebook, and Google* (New York: Penguin Books, 2018)

better than other products! Ugh. I'm getting sleepy just typing these sentences.

Tim Staples drives home the futility of this approach by describing an SRM campaign in which J.Crew simply transmitted their old marketing content through a digital channel. They sent their Facebook followers a video of a vapid-looking young man who asserts that the company paying him to make the ad produces excellent T-shirts. They fit really well, and the cotton is especially soft, so, you know, you should buy one. The result? Exactly one of the 1.8 million recipients shared the video. And the one entry in the comment section consisted of a single word: "Rubbish."

So now consider the example set by the CEO at SAS. He learns about this fiasco and recognizes he's working in a wartime environment. So he decides to be a wartime CEO. He doesn't ask, "What's great about my products?" Instead of focusing on what he wants to sell, he decides to focus on the consumer, on telling a story and building a relationship by providing something of value. He reframes the question: "If I forget about sales for a moment, what application of statistics, analytics, and artificial intelligence might people want to see on the internet?" And he remembers that a division of his company has a project with a conservation group named WildTrack. And what do they do? They're trying to save a number of endangered species across the world: lions, cheetahs, and rhinos in Africa; tigers in India.

Lions and tigers? Or graphs and advertising speak? It's not a hard choice!

He tells his team to make a video focusing on big cats in Namibia—because who can resist a video about stalking lions and racing cheetahs? The video shows exotic African bushmen, experts in tracking these animals. We learn that every individual cat has a footprint as unique as one of our fingerprints. The video mentions that statistics, analytics, and artificial intelligence can encode and refine information about those footprints so scientists can monitor population data and movement patterns, as well as the age, gender, and size of every individual. We see WildTrack scientists using software, but SAS stays wisely in the background—just enough so you might recall the name from the logo that appears without being mentioned in the final second of the video. The software is just a tool, a means to an end. It's a minor character with barely a walk-on part. Nobody is trying to sell anything yet. We're watching a video about wild animals, worrying about their survival, and admiring the people trying to save them. And it's riveting. It's the kind of video you start sharing with friends even before you've finished watching. See for yourself at https://www.jmp.com/en_us/customer-stories/wildtrack.html.

Through this approach, SAS—a North Carolina company—took the first step in forming a genuine relationship with consumers around the world. People will eagerly watch the next installment of this story. And in every subsequent episode, SAS can begin to focus a bit more on its own contributions. It can introduce the tag line: "Using Data for Good." And since the company knows that budding researchers tend to stick with the analytic software they used in school and at the start of their careers, it's establishing lifelong consumers. By using SRM, the company can reach millions of potential buyers. You can't do that with a single commercial during a football or basketball game. And nobody is going to write "Rubbish" in the comments section.

In the next chapter, we'll look at why traditional marketing channels are drying up and what impact this will have on legacy brands. Can they survive? If so, what changes will they need to make? Is Scott Galloway correct when he says Google is "the executioner of brands and media"? Or that "death, for brands, has a name: Alexa"? (Or is it Siri?) In The Impatience Economy, is your new favorite brand whatever Google returns to you in .0000005th of a second? I can guarantee you, it is not!

CHAPTER FOUR

Why Traditional Marketing Channels Are Drying Up

Yellow Pages, Sears Catalogs, and Eastman Kodak

THE DEMISE OF THE YELLOW PAGES IN THE BACK OF THE traditional phone book represents one of the most striking examples of how quickly an essential marketing channel can dry up and vanish, like a water hole on the Sahara's salt road, Azalai. For half a century, consumers sat beside their landlines and combed through the mustard-colored and alphabetized listings of business and services categories—everything from auto dealers and bookstores to yoga instructors and Zamboni repairers. For a minimal fee, a business could display its company's name, address, and phone numbers. More ambitious marketers could buy variously sized advertisements to overshadow their small-print competitors.

In the 1970s, and even 1980s, the ubiquitous five-hundred-page Sears catalog—so thick that tearing it apart was a common strongman stunt—was an innovative "marketing platform" before anyone had ever uttered that phrase. It was a regular part of

American culture, and something everyone could recognize. The Sears catalogue was a big deal. And then it disappeared.

Though it's hard to imagine now, Sears succeeded by taking the first steps down the path that drives today's Second Consumer Revolution: speed, convenience, and expanded consumer choices. Photos of the pneumatic tube station at the company's Chicago mail-order plant must have looked surreal in 1917, when the US was still using horse-drawn artillery to fight World War I. Each worker stares at a bank of ten or more tubes, ready to quickly receive and reroute messages, trying to pack as much productive activity as possible into the 1,440 minutes in a day. As *The Atlantic's* Derek Thompson noted, one of the keys to Sears's success was its insight into how to employ the newly expanded postal service: "Mail was an internet before the internet. After the Civil War, several new communications and transportations systems—the telegraph, rail, and parcel delivery—made it possible to shop at home and have items delivered to your door. Americans browsed catalogues on their couches for jewelry, food, and books. Merchants sent the parcels by rail."[23]

But the Sears catalog could not survive the arrival of the internet and the mobile phone. It suddenly seemed as quaint as smoke signals and talking drums. Nor could it survive the arrival of Walmart, whose more efficient use of technology should be a warning sign and a spur to action for CEOs in 2020. As Thompson says, "The tragic irony of the Sears saga is that communications technology, marshalled so brilliantly during Sears's rise, was instrumental in the company's downfall. In the 1980s, Walmart and other more modern retailers used new digital technology to understand what shoppers were buying and to relay those findings [not by pneumatic tubes] to Walmart headquarters, which could place bulk orders for the new best-selling

[23] Derek Thompson, "The History of Sears Predicts Nearly Everything Amazon Is Doing" (*The Atlantic*, September 25, 2017)

brands and products. With Walmart playing a superior game of sell-cheap-stuff efficiently, Sears's fall was swift. In the early 1980s, it was five times as big as Walmart, by total revenue. By the early 1990s, Walmart was twice as big as Sears." In 2018, Sears filed for bankruptcy.

Companies who fail to appreciate the impact of a new digital era can expect to follow Sears's path. The Eastman Kodak Company invented the digital camera in 1975, but dismissed it as a fad whose output could never compete with its analog, chemically based, silver-nitrate films.[24] The result of this colossal mixture of timidity and hubris? After losing 122,550 jobs, the company founded by George Eastman in 1888 filed for bankruptcy on January 19, 2012.[25] The names of the CEOs who presided over that downfall live on in infamy in Rochester, New York, whose economy was decimated by their myopia. Videos of the orderly implosion of more than ninety of the company's buildings—filmed, ironically, on digital cameras—make for painful YouTube viewing.[26]

But no number of heartrending TV ads about taking photos of junior and cute little sis (they grow up so fast!) were going to keep customers buying film and waiting days to see a single (and perhaps out-of-focus) copy of the results, when they could take as many photos as they wanted at no cost, and instantly post multiple copies on Facebook, Instagram, and other social media feeds for all their friends to see. Digital users could even crop and doctor the images (again, on their phones) to present themselves in the most favorable light. In the end, the backlit cell phone screen replaced the photo album as the repository of our memories. And no one outside of Rochester longs for the good old days.

---

[24] Paul Snyder, *Is This Something George Eastman Would Have Done? The Decline and Fall of Eastman Kodak Company* (Scotts Valley California: CreateSpace Independent Publishing Platform, 2013)

[25] John J. Larish, *Out of Focus: The Story of How Kodak Lost Its Direction* (Scotts Valley California: CreateSpace Independent Publishing Platform, 2012)

[26] See, for example, "Kodak Building 23 Implosion," https://www.youtube.com/watch?v=2JZGm_a1ANkhttps://www.youtube.com/watch?v=2JZGm_a1ANk

Crumbling Foundations

One reason traditional *marketing* channels are drying up is almost tautological: traditional *media* channels have been steadily evaporating. To see the first arrival signs of the Second Consumer Revolution, look at the shift in average daily time spent with digital versus traditional media over the past decade.[27]

- Digital media use jumped from three hours and fifty-six minutes in 2011 to seven hours and thirty-one minutes in 2020, an increase of 111 percent.
- Traditional media use (e.g., television, radio, newspapers, magazines) declined by 20 percent (i.e., more than 1.5 hours) over that same interval.

The trends highlighted in the graph below are likely to intensify in the foreseeable future. Alvin Toffler's *Future Shock* (1970), James Gleick's *Faster* (1999), and Peter H. Diamandis and Steven Kotler's *The Future Is Faster Than You Think* (2020) all chronicle, at twenty-year intervals, the relentlessly shocking acceleration of digital media.

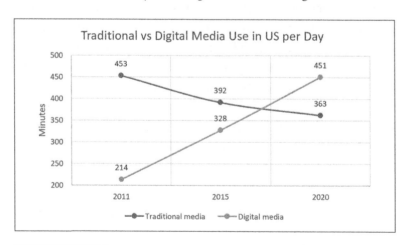

[27] Amy Watson, "Time spent with digital vs. traditional media in the US, 2011-2020, *Statista*, June 17, 2020 (https://www.statista.com/statistics/565628/time-spent-digital-traditional-media-usa/)

Changes in media preferences—driven by consumer demands for increased convenience—have fueled this acceleration. Metaphorically speaking, the oats that powered our old horses are being replaced by gasoline and nuclear power. Animal lovers may keep horses in their picturesque back pasture and mount up for a relaxing weekend jaunt, but they've stopped riding them to work.

Scott Galloway, entrepreneur and professor of marketing at NYU Stern School of Business, asserts that "any retailer that wants to double its revenue in the next five years has to figure out a way to get into a *monogamous* relationship with the consumer and into a recurring revenue model."[28] Traditional media can't achieve that goal. A one-size-fits-all broadcasting approach creates impersonal *polygamous* relationships with generalized composite consumers. The SRM model, on the other hand, aims to establish precisely the one-to-one relationship that Galloway extols.

Desktops versus Mobile Phones in 2020

Having shown that digital media are outpacing traditional media, let's take a more granular look at the former category as of 2020. What's most striking here is the shift in time spent on mobile devices as compared that on desktop computers—and the widening range of business and social activities conducted by phone.[29]

- Companies today spend over 50 percent of their total advertising budget on digital and social campaigns on Facebook and Google.[30]
- In the three months of the extreme COVID-19 lockdowns, e-commerce penetration growth matched that of the

---

[28] Robyn Smith, "Top brand strategist Scott Galloway breaks down retail trends," *Business of Home Magazine*, February 1, 2019

[29] Much of the data below comes from Christo Pertrov, "Mobile vs. Desktop Usage Statistics for 2020: Mobile's Overtaking! (techjury, August 11, 2020, https://techjury.net/blog/mobile-vs-desktop-usage/)

[30] wearesocial.com, Digital 2020 Global Digital Overview

previous ten years, growing from 5.6 percent in 2009, to 16 percent in 2019, to 33 percent in April of 2020.[31]

- By 2021, mobile purchases are predicted to be worth $3.56 trillion—72.9 percent of all e-commerce. In 2016, those figures were lower than $1 trillion (amounting to 58.9 percent of all-commerce) but have increased at a steady rate every year since then.[32]
- By the end of 2020, 70 percent of all B2B inquiries will be made by phone.

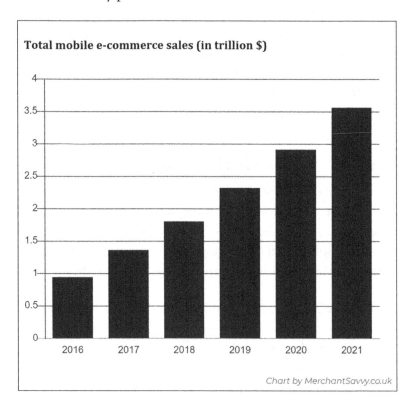

Total mobile e-commerce sales (in trillion $)

Chart by MerchantSavvy.co.uk

---

[31] Periscope by McKinsey, *Retail Reimagined: The New Era for Customer Experience,* August 2020

[32] Global Mobile e-Commerce Statistics, Trends, and Forecasts(MerchantSavvy. co.uk)

- Millennials (i.e., 24–34-year-olds) spend three hours and twenty-four minutes per day on their phones.
- Mobile devices account for more than 70 percent of YouTube viewing.[33]
- Phone-based costs per click (CPC) are 24 percent lower than desktop CPCs and have a 40 percent higher click-through rate (i.e., consumers are more engaged).
- As of October 2019, there were over four billion unique mobile internet users.
- Mobile devices account for 98 percent of the time spent on Facebook, 85 percent of the time spent on Twitter, and 65 percent of the time spent on LinkedIn.[34]
- Over 50 percent of video consumption takes place on mobile devices.

One of the constraints to even wider mobile usage has been connection speed. As we move to enhanced 5G capacity, that constraint will be drastically reduced. Speeds 100 times greater than 4G will exponentially increase connections among consumers, machines, and industries. And consumer growth will skyrocket. From 2017 to 2025, the number of digitally connected users will rise from 3.8 billion[35] to 8.2 billion,[36] an increase of an astounding 116 percent.

[33] Kate Dreyer, "Comscore Enhances Mobile Video Reporting for YouTube and Its Partner Channels to Bolster Cross-Platform Measurement" (Comscore.com, February 23, 2017)

[34] Ana Gotter, "38 Mobile Marketing Statistics You Need to Know" (*Business 2 Community*, https://www.business2community.com/marketing/38-mobile-marketing-statistics-you-need-to-know-02185085)

[35] See The World Bank, "Individuals using the internet (% of population)," https://data.worldbank.org/indicator/IT.NET.USER.ZS

[36] Daniel Goodkind, "The World Population at 7 Billion" (US Census Bureau, October 31, 2011 https://www.census.gov/newsroom/blogs/random-samplings/2011/10/the-world-population-at-7-billion.html)

Diamandis and Kotler refer to these users as "the rising billions."[37] They point out that most of these people won't be visiting brick-and-mortar stores, but will make their purchases from mobile phones: "To put this in broader terms, because retail is nestled at the convergence of communications, energy, and transportation breakthroughs, it's a canary in a coal mine, ground zero for the . . . 'next major economic paradigm shift.' And one thing's for certain, shopping will never be the same."[38]

Mobile Phones and Social Retail Marketing

If the movement from traditional to digital media began to evaporate the old marketing water holes, the increase in mobile phone use (compared to desktop use) is leaving them bone dry. That's because a substantial and rapidly growing fraction of online usage is spent on social media—about one of every five minutes—and most users now access social channels exclusively on their phones. Indeed, 91 percent of all internet users have mobile accounts; for social media users, the figure is 98 percent.[39]

[37] Peter H. Diamandis and Steven Kotler, *Abundance: The Future Is Better than You Think*, (New York: Simon and Shuster, 2014)

[38] Peter H. Diamandis and Steven Kotler, *The Future Is Faster Than You Think: How Converging Technologies Are Transforming Business, Industries, and Our Lives* (New York: Simon and Shuster, 2020)

[39] Luke Pensworth, "Why Digital Media Is Killing TV Advertising" (*Hubspot.com*, February 18, 2020)

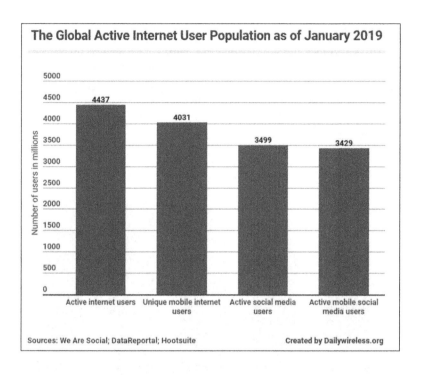

The Global Active Internet User Population as of January 2019

Sources: We Are Social; DataReportal; Hootsuite   Created by Dailywireless.org

School and work activities remain the province of desktops and laptops, but social media consumption seems to require a portable device. Indeed, by 2021, more than 54 percent of social media users will be mobile only.[40] And as we saw in Chapter 3, traditional marketing methods perform dismally on social media platforms.

Social media use is expanding across the globe. As of July 2020, there were 3.91 billion active users worldwide.[41] That amounts to fifty percent of the entire global population. As internet access and mobile phone use expand, that number is expected to reach 4.41 billion by 2025.[42] And since typical users spend two hours and twenty-four

---

[40] Blake Droesch, "More Than Half of US Social Media Users Will Be Mobile-Only in 2019" (eMarketer.com, April 26, 2019)

[41] J. Clement, "Mobile Social Media: Statistics and Facts" (*Statistica*, August 20, 2019)

[42] J. Clement, "Number of Global Social Network Users, 2017 to 2025 (*Statistica*, July 15, 2020)

minutes per day on social media, businesses will have plenty of opportunities to establish relationships with them. Usage varies from country to country. In the US, the figure is one hour and fifty-seven minutes; in the Philippines, it's four hours and one minute.

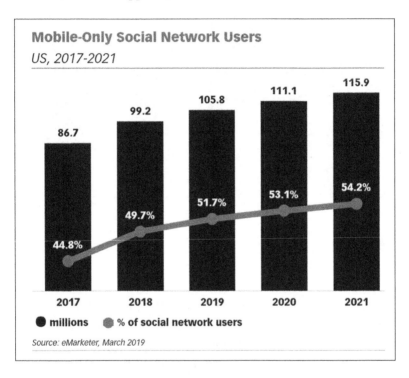

Mobile-Only Social Network Users
US, 2017-2021

- 2017: 86.7 million, 44.8%
- 2018: 99.2 million, 49.7%
- 2019: 105.8 million, 51.7%
- 2020: 111.1 million, 53.1%
- 2021: 115.9 million, 54.2%

● millions   ● % of social network users

Source: eMarketer, March 2019

Few consumers spend a comparable amount of time viewing traditional marketing: How long does it take to drive past a billboard? How long before some graffiti artist turns it into an obscenity? Who really engages with magazines designed to be skimmed rather than read (have you looked at the vapid, sloppily written, more or less unreadable remnant of *Sports Illustrated* lately)? Why rush home to watch a TV program at its scheduled 7:00 p.m. airtime, when all content is available for streaming whenever you want—and you can use the slider bar or the thirty-second-jump button to replay what you didn't understand or skip past commercials and guests you don't like?

In what sense is the show even a TV program anymore when a more consumer-friendly and editable version of the same show is always accessible by phone and impervious to advertisement? What is the point of expensive commercials when fewer and fewer people watch TV and 86 percent of those who do mute the sound, change the channel, or leave the room rather than endure them—and 75 percent find the traditional content manipulative and unreliable?[43] Why return to the same dry water holes? They aren't going to magically refill. Why not shift to the expanding watershed of social media? We know that 71 percent of consumers are more likely to make a purchase based on information received from these channels than from traditional ones.

And consider this: although the figures on social media use are already impressive, the growth potential remains astounding. As J. Clement observes, "Social network penetration is constantly increasing worldwide, and as of January 2019 stood at 45 percent. This figure is anticipated to grow as lesser developed digital markets catch up with other regions when it comes to infrastructure development and the availability of cheap smartphone devices. In fact, most of social media's global growth is driven by the increasing use of mobile devices. The mobile-first market in Eastern Asia topped the global ranking of mobile social networking penetration, followed by established digital powerhouses, such as the Americas and Northern Europe."

---

[43] Mike Ewing, "71% More Likely to Purchase Based on Social Media Referrals" (blog.hubspot,com, June 28, 2019).

Number of social network users in selected countries in 2020 and 2025 (in millions)		
Country	2020	2025
China (mainland)	926.84	1,135.13
India	349.97	409.30
Indonesia	198.96	256.11
United States	223.03	243.42
Brazil	141.45	157.85
Bangladesh	58.77	99.3
Mexico	80.88	95.22
Vietnam	73.56	93.68
Philippines	79.58	90.04
Japan	86.06	89.08
Russia	72.81	75.48
Turkey	54.34	71.44
Thailand	52.72	61.77
United Kingdom	48.63	50.89
South Korea	44.47	45.53
Germany	44.48	45.41
Nigeria	28.15	44.63
France	36.92	38.51
Italy	34.04	36.09

Source: J. Clement, "Social Network Users in Selected Countries in 2020 and 2025" (*Statistica*, July 15, 2020)

Experience Centers versus Immersive Technologies

Providing a distinctive in-store experience is another marketing strategy that—while not drying up completely—is about to undergo a radical and democratizing change. People will probably continue to visit Apple stores for the atmospherics—for the experience of seeing new products and for the self-flattering sense of being hip, successful, and tech savvy. They'll continue to visit Tesla stores for the same reasons—and for the chance to observe, touch, and test-drive Elon Musk's latest creations. But how many brands or industries have the flair or the money to create such experiences? How often would attempting to do so even make sense?

Who wants to bask in a Toyota showroom? Is Lowe's or Home Depot going to increase its market share by investing in an aromatherapy campaign (lavender-scented chainsaw aisles?) or by artfully arranging its weed trimmers and floor tiles—and then hanging up giant high-priced, overdesigned posters of pouting or ruggedly handsome home-repair models, as if it were the Gap? When you decide to buy a ceiling fan, do you care about ambiance? Do you need to smell-test a fifty-pound bag of cow manure before spreading it across for your backyard garden?

But what happens when Lowe's is the first to provide a time-saving and immersive experience that lets you know exactly how much fertilizer you need to cover that garden and the hard-to-measure area around your shrubs—or lets you see how red roses might compare with yellow roses or geraniums in the window planters beside your beige-colored house? What happens when a new clothing store connects to your social media feed, and allows you to try on and compare every shirt they make (not just the ones stocked in the closest mall) so that you know precisely how each one looks and feels as you walk around your living room? Suddenly a thirty-minute drive to a crowded parking lot seems a steep price to pay for a bit of rap music, fancy decor, and the always uncomfortable experience of confronting a salesperson paid on commission.

Various immersive technologies have already appeared— some requiring nothing more than your mobile phone, others requiring goggles and skin sensors. All of them give companies a competitive advantage over their rivals by doing what we described in Chapter 3: *offering the consumer something of value.* Home Depot, Lowe's, and IKEA all now offer mobile augmented-reality (AR) technologies that enable consumers to see how tables, faucets, and other items look in their own homes.[44] Timberland has created a virtual fitting room, and StubHub delivers a 3D model of stadiums so sports fans can view the field from various seats before deciding how much they want to pay for tickets—a shift that increased customer engagement by more than 50 percent within a single year. Though these venture into what is sometimes called "retailtainment," and the "Spatial Web" may sound like science fiction, CEOs ignore them at their peril. Best practices are still being refined, but 53 percent of consumers already say they are more likely to recall products that engage them with immersive technologies. They say that they feel a deeper sense of connection to such businesses—two of the central pillars of Social Retail Marketing. Studies also show that AR engages consumers' attention for eighty-five seconds, increases interaction rates by 20 percent, and improves click-through rates to purchase by 33 percent.[45] [46]

Do I need more data to convince you that AR should be part of your SRM strategy? Consider the following statistics:[47]

- 61 percent of consumers prefer retailers who offer AR over those who don't.
- 68 percent of consumers spend more time considering a product if AR is available.

[44] Caroline Forsey, "Eight Innovative and Inspiring Examples of Augmented Reality in Marketing (blog.hubspot.com, August 28, 2020)

[45] "Try it. Trust it. Buy it: Opening the door to the next wave of digital commerce" (Accenture.com)

[46] "Nine Case Studies That Prove Experiential Retail Is the Future" (the storefront. com, September 24, 2019)

[47] The numbers in all three bullets are from Marketing Using Virtual and Augmented Reality (SmartInsight.com)

- 72 percent of shoppers make unplanned purchases because of AR.

If traditional marketing methods are drying up, immersive technologies are starting to erupt like geysers. Enhanced 5G capacity and latency performance will make AR even more accessible and real: 5G offers speeds 100 times greater than 4G and with latency below ten milliseconds (i.e., faster than the one hundred milliseconds it takes images to travel from our eyes to our brains). Worldwide, there were fewer than five hundred million AR users in 2015; by 2023, that number will reach 2.5 billion, a 400 percent increase. That growth has occurred, in part, from improved convenience. There was plenty to improve on: the first AR headset—developed at Harvard in 1968—had to be fastened to the ceiling and was called "The Sword of Damocles," a phrase taken from an ancient Roman tale in which a king sits (uneasily) beneath a giant guillotine-like blade suspended by a single horsehair, ready to break at his slightest misstep. Like to try it on?

Fortunately, modern versions have become progressively less life-threatening. Multimedia journalist Julianne Pepitone says, "Virtual reality technology is evolving from merely strapping on a headset for a visual encounter to truly immersive experiences incorporating every human sense. This type of VR experience not only makes you feel like you're in a different world—it also tricks the most primal parts of your brain into believing it. Your higher consciousness might know you're standing in a VR kiosk in a mall, but your senses see, hear, feel and even smell a completely different environment." Tico Ballagas, senior manager in Hewlett-Packard's Artificial Intelligence and Emerging ComputeLab, adds, "One of the high-level ideas floating out there, even outside of VR, is that we're entering a new age. We shifted from the Industrial

Age to the Information Age, and now we're transitioning to the Experience Age."[48]

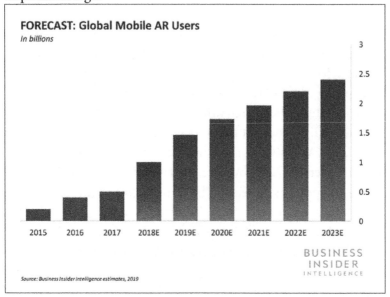

FORECAST: Global Mobile AR Users
In billions

Source: Business Insider Intelligence estimates, 2019

BUSINESS INSIDER INTELLIGENCE

Entrenchment and the Fate of Brands

Investors are divided on what these changes will mean for brands. Some see them as a boon, on the assumption that established businesses will use the new technologies to expand their market share. Others see them as a death knell. They point out that search engines, user reviews, and digital assistants (e.g., Microsoft's Cortana, Alibaba's Tmall Genie, Google's Assistant, Apple's Siri, and Amazon's Alexa) have drained the emotion out of purchasing decisions: if your assistant has proven as trustworthy as an old English butler (e.g., P. G. Wodehouse's Jeeves) and you tell him you need a pair of jeans, and he then orders something of equal or superior quality (at an equal or cheaper price) to the Levi's you've worn all your life, you'll stop caring about Levi's. And there's

---

[48] Julianne Pepitone, "Virtual Reality's New Tricks: How It Fools Your Brain into Having a 'Real' Experience" (Hewlett Packard: The Garage, August 13, 2019)

data to support this view: since 2008, the number of people who can identify a favorite fashion brand has declined by 20 percent. NYU's Scott Galloway is the most articulate and cutting proponent of the death-knell view:

> Many of my colleagues in academia and business believe that brand building will always be a winning strategy. They're mistaken. Of the thirteen firms that outperformed the S&P five years in a row (yes, there's just thirteen), only one of them is a consumer brand—Under Armour [and it was off the list in 2017]. Creative execs at ad agencies and brand managers at consumer firms may soon "decide to spend more time with their families." The sun has passed midday on the brand era.

My own view is more nuanced. I don't agree that brands are doomed—unless they fail to meet the challenge of The Impatience Economy. Laggard brands will certainly be culled from the herd. They will feel increasing competition from small businesses, who couldn't compete for Super Bowl ads but *can* compete on social media—a big plus for consumers. And brands accustomed to winning simply by showing up are in for a rude awakening. Or a quick euthanasia.

One challenge for brands will be a willingness to take the long view. That may require weathering short-term setbacks as they transition to SRM. But you can't cross the Sahara to the life-giving waters of the Mediterranean by retreating when you're halfway there. Your journey will be the same distance, but you'll end up back in the same untenable place you began. Reaching the other side will require top-down support and a willingness to enforce difficult wartime decisions, firing entrenched generals who defend the status quo and replacing them with young, energetic, creative, forward-thinking warriors. Difficult times demand difficult choices. Do you want to blacken some eyes and survive? Or politely lay down and die?

Like it or not, those are your choices. Brands that adapt will survive. Those who won't (or can't) keep up with the customer-centric changes required by The Impatience Economy had better start preparing to cross the business equivalent of the River Styx to join the underworld shades of Kodak, Sears, Motorola, Nokia, and Macy's. In "From Sparta," James Finnegan frames this challenge more eloquently than I can. And he does so in terms of this chapter's governing metaphor, the dried-up water hole:

> We're not heroes, we're soldiers.
> If you thirst, turn back your tears.
> The next well is a day's march from here.

I'll close with two analogies—the first, from business, and the second, from poetry.

More than five billion people have mobile phones. Mobile purchases account for over 70 percent of all e-commerce. That's over $3.5 trillion. What percentage of that figure goes to phone companies?

Basically zero.

Why? Because they didn't pay attention. For more than thirty years, mobile phones have essentially been glued to billions of consumers, twenty-four hours per day, sitting in their pockets and on their nightstands, riding shotgun in their cars, even following them into the bathroom. But the phone companies have never paid attention to what those consumers want. So along came Facebook and Amazon, and because they weren't entrenched in the status quo, they used the phone companies and their networks to offer the consumer an experience, a relationship, and a community through social media. And the mobile phone companies got left behind. The very industry that I helped create globally got left out in the cold.

Businesses that cling to traditional sales and marketing channels are making the same mistake. If they listen to their old-school marketing departments, if they continue to make TV, radio, and print ads, if they persist in crawling back to the same empty water holes, they are going to pay a terrible price. An enormous opportunity is presenting itself, but they will waste their potential and die in the dark unless they rise to the challenge of The Impatience Economy.

In "Le Guignon," Charles Baudelaire captures a sense of this waste:

"Many a gem," the poet mourns," abides
forgotten in the dust,
unnoticed there;

"many a rose" regretfully confides
the secret of its scent
to empty air.[49]

Don't let that be your business epitaph. You can shape your future, or you can die in the "empty air." The choice is yours.

In the next chapter, we'll look more closely at The Impatience Economy and the increased power consumers will have over what, when, where, and how they consume products and services. We'll mark the end of the era when Steve Jobs could say, "People don't know what they want until you show it to them" and the start of an era where consumers not only assert what they want, but also demand to have it instantaneously. We'll explore the synergistic and sustainable power of connecting what will soon be 8.2 billion mobile and social media consumers with all the players in

---

[49] Charles Baudelaire, *Les Fleurs du Mal,* translated by Richard Howard (Boston: David R. Godine Publisher, 2008)

the digital ecosystem. And we'll see how Social Retail Marketing can responsibly offer consumers instant, contextual, and relevant goods and services to help shape their experiences and meet their needs and desires.

CHAPTER FIVE

Power to the Consumer

The Consumer Is No Fool!

P. T. Barnum's (probably apocryphal) "There's a sucker born every minute" and H. L. Mencken's (probably apocryphal) "No one ever went broke underestimating the intelligence of the American public" encapsulate the open, unabashed, almost boastful contempt of an earlier generation's view of the consumer. The quips are still funny, no matter who coined them. But they are no longer true.

Today, only a sucker underestimates the intelligence of the socially connected buyer. "These are the best-informed, most-connected target audiences we've ever marketed to," Nortel Networks' CMO Laureen Flaherty tells *The Economist*. "And I think [a company's success] is going to be a test of who respects that versus who doesn't."[50]

In "We're all connected: The power of the social media ecosystem," researchers are more specific: "Consumers are no longer merely passive recipients in the marketing exchange process.

---

[50] *The Economist*: Future Tense: The Global CMO—A Report from The Economist Intelligence Unit, 2008 (http://graphics.eiu.com/upload/Google%20Text.pdf)

Today, they are taking an increasingly active role in co-creating everything from product design to promotional messages."[51]

In this chapter, we'll explore how power shifted from producers to consumers and the implications of that shift in the modern marketplace.

How Social Media Empowers the Consumer

As we saw in Chapter 4, digital consumers have a greater range of choices than did their pre-internet ancestors. The SRM approach levels the playing field for small businesses that could simply not compete in the high-dollar arena where pricey TV commercials or glossy ads in *GQ* and *Vanity Fair* were the primary avenues for shaping purchasing decisions. Now that every resourceful company or mom-and-pop shop can access billions of consumers through social media feeds, big brands can no longer dictate the rules of the game. As Nobel Prize–winning economist Joseph E. Stiglitz asserts, this shift serves the consumer's interests:

> Competition is an essential feature of a successful economy, driving firms to be efficient and driving down prices. Competition limits the power of market actors to tip economic and political outcomes in their favor.
>
> With many firms competing, no single one has the power to raise prices and its own profits because customers can buy from any number of competitors.[52]

---

[51] Richard Hanna, Andrew Rohm, Victoria L. Crittenden, "We're all connected: The power of the social media ecosystem (Indiana University, Kelley School of Business, *Elsevier*, Volume 54, May 2011)

[52] Joseph E. Stiglitz, *Rewriting the Rules of the American Economy: An Agenda for Growth and Shared Prosperity* (New York: W.W. Norton and Company, 2016)

This is precisely what Social Retail Marketing is accomplishing. Today's consumers expect more choices, better quality, and faster service than ever before. They expect sellers to come to them—rather than the other way around. Most crucially, consumers have the power to *enforce* these expectations. They can punish any seller in the digital ecosystem based on their actions—or inactions. Simply making a quality product is no longer enough. It's a *necessary* condition—but not a *sufficient* one—for making a sale. You can make the world's best lemonade, but if you set up your stand on the median of a busy interstate, you might as well be selling cups of tepid vinegar.

In the current market, you can go out of business for missteps a lot less severe than forcing thirsty customers to risk being run over by a truck. By failing to take the consumer's point of view, many businesses are making the lemonade-stand mistake—only in less spectacularly flamboyant ways. But in practice, the result will be the same: anything that slows down or complicates the buying process—that disrupts the customer's pursuit of convenience—will be a deal-breaker. For businesses that fail to appreciate this change, the term *seller* will quickly become a misnomer—because they are not going to be making any sales. Today, the governing principle is not *caveat emptor* (i.e., *buyer* beware), but *caveat venditor* (i.e., *seller* beware).

In *The Cluetrain Manifesto*, the authors speak in the voice of a frustrated consumer who rejects traditional sales approaches:

> Conversations are the "products" the new markets are "marketing" to one another constantly online.
>
> By comparison, corporate messaging is pathetic. It's not funny. It's not interesting. It doesn't know who we are, or care. It only wants us to buy. If we wanted more of that, we'd turn on the tube. But we don't, and we won't. We're too busy. We're too wrapped up in some fascinating conversation.

Engagement in these open free-wheeling market-place exchanges isn't optional. It's a prerequisite to having a future. Silence is fatal.[53]

Thus speaks the socially connected consumer.

It's What You Didn't Do

In considering modern market dynamics, I'm reminded of a popular country-and-western song, "What I Didn't Do," sung by Steve Wariner.[54] Having been abruptly dumped by his wife or girlfriend (of course! It's country music), the puzzled Wariner begins by recounting his virtues ("I didn't cheat. I didn't lie."), much as a failed business might point to its quality products and lament, "How could consumers reject them?" But Wariner quickly realizes his failures have been those of *omission* rather than of *commission:*

> I didn't tell her each day I loved her.
> I took it for granted, somehow she knew.
> I didn't hold her when she needed a shoulder.
> It's not what I did. It's what I didn't do.

Business executives who don't want to be humming this tune while updating their LinkedIn profiles (and trying to disguise the failure that has placed them back in the job market) need to adjust to changing consumer expectations in patience Economy.

When describing this seismic shift, I'm not just basing my views on a few personal experiences or anecdotes. It's been well

---

[53] R. Levine, C. Locke, D. Searle, and D. Weinberger(2001), *The Cluetrain Manifesto: The End of Business As Usual* (New York: Basic Books, 2001)
[54] The song was written by Wood Newton and Michael Noble and released in 1984 on Wariner's *One Good Night Deserves Another* (https://youtu.be/OwogoGQmoFU)

documented in academic literature. S. Umit Kucuk, for example, points out the following:

> The internet introduced the most democratic market structure and consumer-company relationship we have seen since before the Industrial Revolution. It is clear that consumers are not solely consuming media as in pre-digital times, but instead they are actively using media to raise their voices and actively involving themselves in markets in order to make economic and social impacts. The internet has empowered consumers in unprecedented ways and levels.[55]

Similarly, in "The Emergence of the Social Media Empowered Consumer," Clodagh O'Brien concludes, "Businesses can no longer simply publish content they wish potential customers to see; the social media landscape has instigated a power shift from the business toward the consumer."[56] He adds that empowered consumers are "increasingly demanding" and can punish businesses that cling to old marketing models rather than establishing a "bidirectional social bond." R. Garretson makes a related point: "Consumers increasingly use digital media not just to research products and services, but to engage the companies they buy from, as well as other consumers who may have valuable insights."[57]

---

[55] S. Umit Kucuk, "Can Consumer Power Lead To Market Equalization On The Internet?" (*Journal of Research for Consumers*, Issue 21, 2012)

[56] Clodagh O'Brien, "The Emergence of the Social Media Empowered Consumer" (*Irish Marketing Review*, Volume 21, 2011)

[57] R. Garretson, "Future tense: The global CMO," September 29, 2010, (http://graphics.eiu.com/upload/Google%20Text.pdf)

The Shift in Consumer Power under Traditional Marketing Approaches versus SRM	
Traditional Marketing	*Social Retail Marketing*
The company is in control.	The consumer is in control.
Business is better for the company.	Business is better for the consumer.
Consumers are treated as segments.	Consumers are treated as unique individuals.
Businesses tell consumers what they think they want.	Consumers tell businesses what they care about.
Customers feel stalked and spammed.	Customers feel empowered.
The focus is on products and services.	The focus is on consumers.
Source: F, Newell, *Why CRM Doesn't Work: How to Win by Letting Customers Manage the Relationship*, (London: Kogan Page, 2003)	

In "Consumer Power: Evolution in the Digital Age," the authors identify four specific ways in which social media has strengthened the consumer's position in the marketplace.[58]

1. *Demand-based power* has eliminated geographic and time constraints, increased buying options, and—through consumer access to more and more distribution centers—driven down prices. Without leaving their social media feeds, consumers have instant access to a wider range of goods, from a wider range of merchants, at cheaper prices. And purchases can be quickly processed without leaving the social media channel. It's a buyer's paradise.

---

[58] Lauren A. Labrecque, Jonas von dem Esche, Charla Mathwick, Thomas P. Novak, and Charles F. Hofacker, "Consumer Power: Evolution in the Digital Age" (*Journal of Interactive Marketing*, Volume 27, pages 257-269, October 17, 2013)

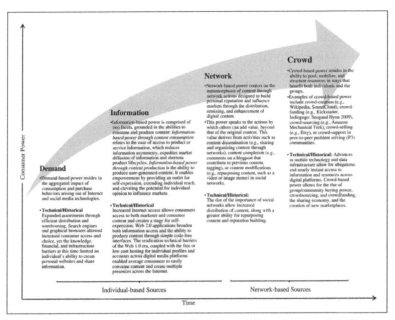

The cascading growth of a social-media consumer's power over time (Lauren A. Labrecque et al.)

2. *Information-based power* reduces knowledge asymmetries between buyers and sellers. Social media users have instant access to product reviews, performance data, and prices—all of which allow them to make more informed choices.

3. *Network-based power* enables each social media user to amplify her individual concerns to thousands of other like-minded consumers.

4. *Crowd-based power* allows consumers to act in concert for their collective benefit and to force sellers into direct competition in ways that serve consumer interests. As James Surowiecki specifies in *The Wisdom of Crowds,* "Large groups of people are often *smarter* than an elite few, no matter how brilliant—better at solving problems, coming to wise decisions, even predicting the future."[59]

---

[59] James Surowiecki, *The Wisdom of Crowds* (New York: Random House, 2005)

A number of surveys have shown that social media boosts consumer power by holding businesses accountable, both for what they do—and fail to do:[60]

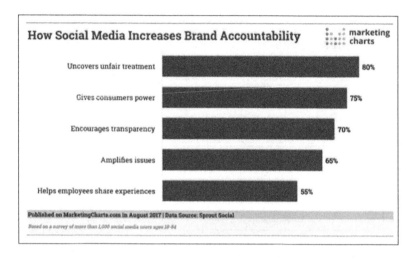

- 75 percent of consumers on social media feel the platform has empowered them to demand brand accountability.
- 60 percent have called out brands for false or misleading claims.
- 59 percent have reported poor customer service.
- 57 percent have reported rudeness.
- 65 percent say they consider complaints by others on social media and then conduct follow-up research before making a purchase.
- 1 in 6 won't buy from a business that has received a complaint on social media.
- 35 percent would boycott a business that fails to respond to a complaint.
- 45 percent would post about a positive response to a complaint.

---

[60] These results are based on a survey of 1,000 US social media users, ages 18 to 64. See "Social Media Gives Consumers Power to Increase Brand Accountability" at marketingcharts.com, August 25, 2017.

The App Trap

One clear-cut expression of consumer power is the steadily increasing rejection of the app. In the abstract, many are puzzled by this trend. How could the unassuming app icon be a pain point or a source of inconvenience? But in that same abstract, many people with email and a mobile phone thought texting would be a redundancy, a colossal flop. Who wants to type a note on a tiny keyboard in the palm of your hand when you could just call someone? Just about everyone. Experience proved the naysayers wrong. What looked like a bad idea in the boardroom turned out to be just what consumers wanted. The same will prove true (in reverse) for those who see the app as a durable fixture on our portable phones. In The Impatience Economy, the extra clicks required to exit the London Review of Books app—where you've been reading a glowing essay about J. K. Rowling's new novel—and open the Amazon app to search for and buy the book has become an Odyssean ordeal—the difference between hauling a water bucket from a distant well and turning on a tap in your kitchen. Strong-willed survivalists and your former-Marine uncle who runs ten miles every morning may bemoan such laziness, but the facts speak for themselves. TVs no longer make you stand up, walk three feet, and manually change the dial. We take the escalator, not the stairs.

The mortality rate for apps has started to exceed the birth rate. In the wild, we'd call that an extinction spiral. Apps are the passenger pigeons of the digital ecosystem. And the number one reason people are rejecting apps? Just what we'd expect in The Impatience Economy: they are too "time-consuming," they are "too complicated to bother with," and they annoy the consumer with "too many ads and notifications."[61] Consumers

---

[61] Cooper Smith, "Here's Why Some Consumers Don't Like Using Shopping Apps" *Business Insider*, April 11, 2014

may tolerate a certain level of complexity on their desktop computer. But the exit threshold is far lower on a mobile phone. Busy people on the move simply won't tolerate complex interfaces or the ordeal of a complex sign-in/registration gauntlet.

Nonetheless, firms continue to invest enormous amounts of time and treasure in app development. This strikes me as self-destructive and financially perverse. It's like carefully washing and waxing your car and then pulling the plug on the oil sump before you go for a drive. The second action makes a mockery of the first. So does investing R&D funds in building a high-quality product and then using an app as your primary marketing channel. The customer may want your product, but she doesn't want your app, so you end up in the self-defeating position of a man trying to fill a barrel that has one short stave. He's wasting his time. The thing won't hold water, and neither will your app-based marketing plan.

Keep in mind the cost of app development in 2020:[62]

- A simple app will set you back $60,000 to $100,000.
- A medium-complexity app will run from $100,000 to $250,000.
- For feature-rich, highly complex apps, the range can be in the tens of millions of dollars, and many large enterprises have spent over $100 million just to take major write-offs once they figured out that an app as a primary reach, sell, and serve marketing channel doesn't work.

The old adage is that *you get what you pay for*. My contention is that—for the typical business, building the typical app—that old bromide should be inverted: *you're paying for something you don't get.*

---

[62] "How Much Does It Cost to Make An App?" (https://www.goodfirms.co/resources/mobile-app-development-cost)

I'll ask you to pause here and look at your own phone. I'm willing to bet the proceeds of this book that one of two things is true: either you routinely purge apps from your screen or you are staring at an overloaded mess of icons you never open. Both could be true. The data suggests I'm going to win this bet.

- The average lifespan (i.e., time to deletion) of a mobile app is 5.8 days.[63]
- 30 percent of Android apps are deleted fewer than ten minutes after they are downloaded; for iPhones, the rate is only a bit lower.[64]
- 70 percent of consumers do not return to an app the day after installing it; 88 percent don't return two weeks later.[65]
- More than 50 percent of apps get deleted because they are memory hogs; they simply take up too much space.
- In 2020, monthly uninstall rates increased 35 percent from 2019.[66]

How much money do apps lose each month because of uninstalls? $33,000. Keep this information in mind as you plan next year's marketing strategy. As I said earlier, *caveat venditor!*

---

[63] "Why People Delete Apps from Their Smartphones," Sigma Telecom, February 13, 2019 (https://sigmatelecom.com/why-do-people-delete-application/)

[64] Hussain Fakhruddin, "Why Do People Uninstall Apps?" January 30, 2016 (https://www.linkedin.com/pulse/top-twelve-reasons-why-users-frequently-uninstall-mobile-apps-fakhruddin)

[65] Rayana Hollander, "Here's how app developers are combating declining retention," Business Insider, 9/12/2017

[66] John Koestler, "App Uninstall Rates and Lockdown," May 21, 2020 (www.singular.net)

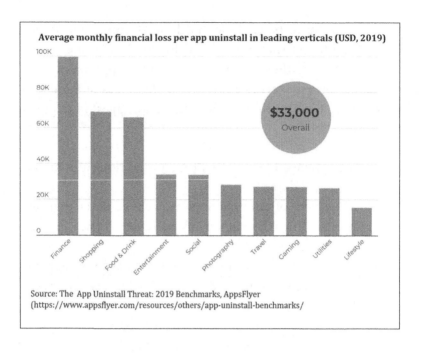

Average monthly financial loss per app uninstall in leading verticals (USD, 2019)

$33,000
Overall

Source: The App Uninstall Threat: 2019 Benchmarks, AppsFlyer
(https://www.appsflyer.com/resources/others/app-uninstall-benchmarks/

Unexpected Social Benefits: From Stove Development to Pandemic Models

Social media can also help open up markets to benefit consumers in unexpected ways. As Nobel Prize–winning economist Michael Kremer points out, across Asia and Africa, millions of people cook by burning wood or using other kinds of stoves that are inconvenient, time-consuming, unhealthy, and environmentally disastrous.[67] Although consumers want alternatives, no one has yet produced a prototype that meets their expectations. These poor consumers have power too. And thus far, they've used it to veto solutions that don't respond to their needs,

Now, as we saw in the last chapter, a huge (and growing) percentage of these people have cell phones and social media

---

[67] From Michael Kremer's dialog on the podcast *Conversations with Tyler* (George Mason University, October 21, 2020) https://podcasts.apple.com/us/podcast/conversations-with-tyler/id983795625?i=1000495536228)

accounts. So rather than wasting money in trying to guess what consumers want, an enterprising business that has established a personal connection with these potential buyers could A/B test various stove models to see why previous attempts have failed. This systematic approach would reduce R&D costs and likely attract advanced marketing commitments[68] from national governments, NGOs, and other philanthropic organizations. These commitments are far more likely to flow to businesses that employ a systematic customer-focused methodology to product development than to those that simply tout the independent genius of their creative staff. Through this process, a business may find that people in West Africa have slightly different preferences from those in South India. Or that consumers fall into several distinct categories—so that the needs of an entire region could be met by providing two or three slightly different models.

So now stove development is guided by consumer preferences and not the ruminations of engineers in a meeting room thousands of miles away. And in the end, whoever solves this problem is doing a lot more than just cashing in on a huge business opportunity. They're doing that, of course, but they are also enhancing the lives of a large fraction of the world's population—both at the individual level and the collective level. And this is just one of thousands of examples of how socially connected consumers will benefit from the shift in buyer-seller power dynamics.

Analyzing social media accounts may also be crucial in helping epidemiologists produce large-scale medical benefits. Two recent studies,[69] [70] for example, suggest that COVID-19 pandemic

---

[68] Funds to help develop a quality product when high R&D costs might hinder such development.

[69] Gianluca Manzo, "Complex Social Networks Are Missing in the Dominant COVID-19 Epidemic Models," *Sociologica,* Volume 1, Number 4, May 22, 2020.

[70] Andrzej Jarynowski, Monika Wójta-Kempa, Daniel Płatek, and Karolina Czopek, "Attempt to understand public health relevant social dimensions of COVID-19 outbreak in Poland," *Social Science Research Network,* April 7, 2020 (Available at SSRN: https://ssrn.com/abstract=3570609 or http://dx.doi.org/10.2139/ssrn.3570609)

models would have been more accurate had developers incorporated information from social networks. In "Complex Social Networks Are Missing in the Dominant COVID-19 Epidemic Models," Gianluca Manzo says current assessments fail to "surgically isolate" specific individuals or groups. He adds, "If complex social networks are seriously considered, more specific interventions can be explored that apply to specific categories or sets of individuals with expected collective benefits."

Andrzej Jarynowski et al. further emphasize the importance of social media in the crisis:

> Recently, the whole of Europe, including Poland, have been significantly affected by COVID-19 and its social and economic consequences, which are already causing dozens of billions of euros in monthly losses in Poland alone. Social behaviour has a fundamental impact on the dynamics of spread of infectious diseases such as SARS-CoV-2, challenging the existing health infrastructure and social organization. Modelling and understanding mechanisms of social behaviour . . . and its contextualization with regard to Poland can contribute to better response to the outbreak on a national and local level.

> We aim to investigate the impact of the COVID-19 on society by measuring the relevant activity in internet news and *social media* . . . to provide urgently needed information on social dynamics during the outbreak.

Both studies decry the failure to use data on mobile phone and social media contacts as a starting point for constructing disease models. Both studies also assert that learning to interpret the data from these networks can produce important public-health benefits for the same groups of socially connected consumers who are the focus of this book. And the vast majority of these users will gladly provide this data because they will receive an unambiguous benefit: increased protection from a potentially life-threatening disease. Once again, networked consumers are empowered in ways that would have been unimaginable in previous generations.

The Social Media Influencer

On social media, an "influencer" is someone who can shape the purchasing decisions of a large group of consumers through regular posts about their area of expertise (e.g., fashion, restaurants, movies, cars). Present on every platform, influencers have been steadily gaining influence and now wield much of the power formerly held by ad agencies—but with this crucial difference: consumers now have the power and freedom to choose whom they follow. Rather than sit through cynical endorsements from some highly paid shill, consumers can choose a like-minded member of their own social community, a trusted peer, someone representing their interests rather than the seller's.

Influencers are the ground troops of the Second Consumer Revolution. "Consumers are too savvy and too bored by endorsements and flat product mentions," says RocketMill's senior creative strategist Bethanie Mardon.[71] "They are influenced by the influencers they choose to follow, largely because they relate to them and trust them." The data support her assertion. Fifty percent of consumers rely on influencer recommendations when deciding which products to buy, and 40 percent have purchased a product after an influencer recommended it on social media.[72]

---

[71] Steven McIntosh, "Influencers: How a New Breed of Social Media Stars Changed the Game" BBC News, April 21, 2019.
[72] Megan Mosley, "Brand Ambassadors vs. Influencers: A Comparison, business2community.com, May 14, 2019

A survey of 1,753 social media influencers revealed that Facebook is the most popular platform, followed by Instagram, Twitter, Pinterest, YouTube, LinkedIn, and Snapchat.[73] And an influencer's most important qualities?

1. Being honest, funny, genuine, and able to form a personal bond with followers
2. Providing value by addressing topics of interest
3. Listening and responding to followers' needs and questions
4. Consistently posting and keeping abreast of what's happening in the market

Able to shape the buying decisions of their followers and the product development decisions of businesses, influencers are a kind of an apex consumer, the tigers of the digital marketplace. They have the power to make or break a business. Companies who work directly with influencers generate an eleven-times-greater return on their investments compared with traditional marketing practices.[74] Companies taken to task by influencers can find themselves looking for new lines of work. As we have seen throughout this chapter, the power has shifted to the consumer.

Compensation for Personal Data

A major change is coming, one in which increasingly empowered consumers will demand—and receive—compensation for the personal data they now give away for free (or for trinkets), and that has driven the astounding growth of Facebook, Google, Amazon, and other tech giants. To date, consumers have been relatively indifferent about this issue. But soon—perhaps *very*

---

[73] Dan Peltier, "Six Charts Showing How Social Media Influencers Work with Brands, Skift, November 29, 2016.
[74] "Ads vs. Influencer Marketing: Which One Works Best?," ProductLead.me, October 2019

soon—they are going to say, "Hey, Mr. Big Shot, I noticed you just sold data about *my* behavior for a whole lot of money. And what did I get out of it? Nada. Zilch. My friends and I are providing you with the energy you need to run your advertising engine. Without us, you're nothing. So how come you keep all the profits?"

As The Impatience Economy develops, this kind of transaction will feel exploitative. As the Old Testament says, you can't make bricks without straw, so (this part isn't in the Bible) if you want bricks, providing straw should be monetized. And consumers are going to insist on that—on owning their own digital identity and having the power to choose who does—or doesn't—get to use their data. There's an old expression, "Money forgets," meaning the guy who makes it often (rather conveniently) doesn't remember who contributed to its acquisition. Socially connected consumers are about to give that guy a stern reminder. That's only fair. As Jaron Lanier says, the idea of paying people for their data "takes capitalism more seriously than it has been taken before. A market economy should not just be about 'businesses,' but about everyone who contributes value."[75]

I like Lanier's concept of "digital dignity." Although there's an element of utopianism in his view, he proposes that we treat user-generated data like labor[76] (i.e., as a production input). That makes us all the commercial owners of whatever can be measured about our behavior:

> In the event that something a person says or does contributes even minutely to a database that allows ... a market-prediction algorithm to perform a task, then a nanopayment—proportional *both* to

[75] Jaron Lanier, *Who Owns the Future?* (New York: Simon and Shuster, 2013)
[76] Imanol Arrieta-Ibarra, Leonard Goff, Diego Jiménez-Hernández, Jaron Lanier, and E. Glen Weyl, "Should We Treat Data as Labor? Moving beyond 'Free,' *American Economic Association Papers and Proceedings*, 108: 38-42, 2013

the degree of the contribution *and* the resultant value—will be due to the person.

Under this model, consumers would have an incentive to act in ways that create value: "These nanopayments will add up and lead to a new social contract in which people are motivated to contribute to an information economy in ever more substantial ways."

And if the current players don't offer that compensation, new players will. No company is safe from revolutionary change. Remember Kodak? Remember MySpace? Do you think the same thing can't happen to Facebook? That it couldn't be disrupted by a company who says, "We are going to take 20 percent of our profits and give consumers a digital-wallet credit for all the data they've provided"? I promise you, people would jump to that platform in a second. Something like that could easily happen to Facebook. *Very* easily.

I'll close this chapter with a quote from *The Economist* concerning both the *ideal* of compensating consumers and the *challenge* of working out the specifics in ways that best serve the interlinked interests of buyers and sellers. In the evolving marketplace, the following is true:

> Each person becomes something like an oil well, pumping out the fuel that makes the digital economy run. Both fairness and efficiency demand that the distribution of income generated by that fuel should be shared more evenly, according to our contributions. The tricky part is working out how.

We'll explore this idea in more depth later in this book. But by now, one thing should be clear: consumers will be sitting at the head of the negotiating table. The power now rests with them.

In the next chapter, we'll get to down to fundamentals. Here are the five rules of successful Social Retail Marketing.

CHAPTER SIX

The Five Rules of Successful Social Retail Marketing™

Step by Step

WHENEVER HE NEEDS A LITTLE INSPIRATION, A BUSIness acquaintance of mine hums an old country song by Eddie Rabbitt called "Step by Step." Something about that cheerful, confident melody transports him to a place where he's ready to resume his work with a revived sense of clarity and creativity. It works for him every time.

Although I won't be bursting into song, my goal in this chapter is to do something similar for you. In detailing the rules to successful SRM, I'm giving you a five-step guide on how to make the creative transition from a traditional marketing approach to the innovative consumer-focused strategy that is the only way to thrive in The Impatience Economy. You can return to these bedrock principles whenever the seductive power of old habits threatens to lure you back to a world that no longer exists. Just as surgeons and pilots internalize a set of optimal procedures to ensure successful outcomes, businesses need to constantly remind themselves of the overarching goals that drive their day-to-day activities. That's especially true during times of rapid change.

I developed these rules through careful observation of—and research into—the shifting patterns of consumer behavior that developed over the past few years, intensified during the COVID-19 pandemic, and have since become the new normal. Recognizing that SRM is the only method suitable to surviving and flourishing in these revolutionary times, I asked myself three questions:

- How can businesses make this new approach work?
- What fundamental strategic changes must they make?
- And what is the best way to implement these changes?

Over time, I distilled my answers to these questions. What follows are the five practical rules that guide all my SRM decisions.

Rule One: Fulfill Consumers' Pursuit of Convenience, Lifestyle, Peace of Mind, and Freedom

In The Impatience Economy, consumers demand convenience: they want fast, frictionless interactions. They want their news instantly, they want responses from their friends instantly, they want digital products instantly, and they want physical products almost instantly—in some cases, within a few hours rather than a day.

Research conducted by Fetch and YouGov shows that modern consumers are unwilling to wait for . . . just about anything. Respondents indicated that technology has made them less patient than they were five years ago.[77] Another study shows that searches for "_____ near me now" have increased by 150 percent over the

---

[77] Ayaz Nanji, "Instant Gratification Nation: The Impatient American Consumer" (marketingprofs.com, August 11, 2017)

last four years.[78] The authors note, "A new breed of consumers has arrived. Empowered by mobile . . . they are more curious, demanding, and impatient than ever before." They conclude that a business's ability to anticipate and quickly respond to those demands will "define its ability to grow."

In the process of writing this book, I often needed reference materials—journal articles on marketing trends, books on consumer behavior, newspaper stories on technological innovations. And I'm as impatient as everyone else. Had I been doing this work several decades ago, I would have spent days driving to college libraries, thumbing through card catalogs, writing down Dewey decimal numbers, and searching through the stacks, hoping that someone hadn't already taken out the one copy of the material I needed—or that it hadn't been misfiled by a librarian or defaced by someone who'd torn out the pages I wanted. I would have brought along a pocket full of coins for the photocopier—and probably would've had to wait in line for the privilege of using it.

Under those conditions, you wouldn't be reading this book. Ever. I would have never found time to write it. Or I would have lost my mind trying.

But ours is an age of convenience. Instead of the various ordeals I just outlined, I used Google and Google Scholar to access, in seconds, much of the material I needed. In just a few minutes, I cut and pasted the quotes I needed into the text you're reading and cited the references. If I needed a particular book, I wasn't about to wait twenty-four hours for some frantic Amazon driver to risk his life and a speeding ticket to knock on my door, forcing me to walk an inconvenient twelve steps to the porch and engage in polite time-wasting banter. Instead, in less than a minute, I was reading the digital version and using the search feature to find the specific passages relevant to my work.

---

[78] "Consumers in the Age of Assistance" (Thinkwithgoogle.com, July 2018)

In other words, my expectations were those of most modern consumers of The Impatience Economy. I demanded access to what I wanted, when I wanted it. Or even sooner. And I'm looking forward to the day when SRM can anticipate what I'll want *before* I want it, as well as eliminating the onerous extra clicks required to open my Amazon app.

All this convenience accords with my pursuit of a new and more enjoyable lifestyle. Not only am I able to work at home or on a plane or from a lounge chair on the beach, but I've also been able to broaden my career. I'm now able to be an author as well as an entrepreneur. I can listen to the latest issue of *The Economist* while driving my car. I can be on my phone doing Zoom calls while sitting outside, enjoying the changing colors of autumn leaves, and—when I want to take a break—order lunch from Uber Eats . . . and a new pair of cowboy boots (I always want more) from Zappos. The possibilities are boundless—all of them convenient, all of them life enriching.

And I get to do this with peace of mind and a sense of freedom because I'm only dealing with businesses I choose to interact with, businesses I trust. I know that my identity is secure, my transactions are safe, and that I'll receive products and services that meet my expectations. In other words, I'm freely choosing convenient, life-enhancing goods and services that bolster my peace of mind—which encompasses all four of the qualities in Rule 1.

Which companies are effectively applying Rule 1? Instead of looking at the usual big-business suspects, let's consider Passport Labs, a small company in Massachusetts: their app, ParkBoston, helps users find parking spaces and avoid tickets by enabling them to add time to the meter from their mobile phones, and automatically transmits that information to parking enforcement officers. As *The Boston Sun* reports, "Gone are the days of quarters. Gone are the days of rushing out of a meeting or during a commercial break to the meter before time expired."[79] Not only is the company's ParkBoston app convenient, it also increases users' freedom and peace of mind by being so reliable; every parking meter in the city has been retrofitted to work with the product. Those qualities have paid big dividends: in the first fourteen months after its release, net monthly revenues jumped from $4,275 to $612,179, an increase of 14,220 percent! Clearly, ParkBoston fulfills consumers' pursuit of convenience, lifestyle, peace of mind, and freedom while boosting its bottom line.

Rule Two: Help Consumers Discover Products and Services They Don't Know Exist

The concept here is akin to reducing what Donald Rumsfeld called—in an admittedly less market-focused context—"unknown unknowns"—those products and services that might enhance people's lives if only they knew what they were missing. Though Rumsfeld is generally considered to have coined the phrase, it actually dates back to a 1955 paper on group dynamics by two American psychologists, Joseph Luft and Harrington Ingham, in which they introduced the "Johari window"—a four-quadrant diagram often used to asses risk (and information imbalances), but which can also be used to identify blind spots and improve mutual understanding in consumer-producer interactions.[80]

Unknown unknowns can be reduced by online social communities that enable participants to explore what is happening in Bangladesh or the Maldives, France or Italy, Jamaica or Brazil. Consumers can quickly learn what people are wearing in Paris or Rome, what they are eating in Bangkok or São Paulo, what music

[79] Seth Daniel, "Park Boston App Surges, Producing Huge Revenue Numbers," *The Boston Sun*, April 29, 2016

[80] Parul Saxena, "Johari Window: An Effective Model for Improving Interpersonal Communication and Managerial Effectiveness" (*SIT Journal of Management*, Volume 5, Number 2, December 2015)

they are listening to in Nashville, or what books they are reading in Stockholm. And on social media, they can discover new ideas, products, and services without being force-fed information they don't want. When you see what might be an interesting product, you take a look without leaving your social media stream, and if you decide it's not for you, you simply click the back arrow and return to the conversation you were having with your friend. You haven't had to open an app, you haven't had to drop out of a dialog and then reconnect. No one is monopolizing your time. You aren't being dragged off by what Tim Wu calls the myriad and annoyingly loud "attention merchants," all competing to get inside our heads, but only managing to increase our resistance.[81]

The whole concept of SRM is that consumers aren't embarking on a strenuous discovery process: they aren't Marco Polo, trudging almost five thousand miles from Venice to the Beijing Han Wall, traversing the (as yet unnamed) Silk Road, dodging the bubonic plague, negotiating deals with Kublai Khan, and returning twenty-four years later with exotic goods from Xanadu. When SRM is done properly, consumers aren't even trying to discover unique products. They make discoveries without searching. They don't have to cross the mountains or risk their lives traversing a desert. They don't even have to drive to the mall or visit a website. They don't have to flip through the Sears catalog to spot a raincoat unlike anything they've ever seen. Consumers aren't Lewis and Clark, willing to face grizzly bears and hostile Sioux as they wander around looking for the athletic-wear equivalent of the Northwest Passage. In The Impatience Economy, consumers expect products to discover *them*. These are the facts. Businesses who can't adjust to them are headed for ruin.

At present, few companies are fully capable of making this adjustment. But those who plan to survive must do so. Consider

---

[81] Tim Wu, *The Attention Merchants: The Epic Scramble to Get Inside Our Heads* (New York: Alfred A. Knoph, 2016)

X Corp Solutions. They do a marvelous job of helping consumers quickly and easily discover new life-enriching products, yet they are still tied to an app. They'll be able to offer an infinitely more rewarding and valuable experience once they migrate to channels inside social media, where consumers spend most of their online time.

Rule Three: Develop a Two-Way Relationship That Is Not Just about Selling, but about Building Trust and Relevance

At first glance, this rule seems counterintuitive: I want to sell something, but I shouldn't focus on selling it? Are you crazy?

No, I'm not. Even in The Impatience Economy, there remains one process that can't be rushed: building a relationship. As evolutionary psychologists will attest, when we are forming bonds, our brains simply won't allow us to compress time. The same is true of acquiring a skill. The guitar novice who practices an hour every day for a month will make far more progress than someone who sits idly for thirty days and then practices for thirty-one hours in a single session.

Imagine you meet a stranger at a party, and the first thing she says is, "Hey, do you want to go to Barcelona with me tomorrow?" or "Do you want to get married?" If you'd established a relationship with each other, your answer to either or both of these questions might be "Yes." But if someone opened with those proposals, not only would you say, "No!" but you'd also start edging away from the questioner. Warning lights would flash. Chances are, you'd never give her another chance to demonstrate whether the two of you might have been compatible. Any possibility of a future relationship is poisoned by the unnatural first encounter. A lion tamer may earn the trust of the king of beasts, but if he's going to demand it on the first encounter, I'd like a chance to take out a life insurance policy on him.

Unfortunately, marketers all too often try to skip the relationship and engagement steps, with the result that the consumer simply moves on to something else. Crucial here is the concept of "priming" as defined by Nobel Prize-winning psychologist Daniel Kahneman—and his collaborator Amos Tversky—in his monumental *Thinking, Fast and Slow*.[82] Particularly important for our purposes is the now well-established notion that purchasing decisions are shaped—to a much larger degree than we are consciously aware—by our experiences just prior to a purchase. Imagine two people of comparable incomes, equally interested in baseball, both Chicago Cubs fans. You might expect that both would be equally responsive to an opportunity to buy tickets to an upcoming game. But you'd be wrong. If, just prior to the offer, Person X had been watching a video about baseball and Person Y had been watching a video about anything else, Person X would be far more likely to buy the ticket. He'd be "primed" to buy a ticket in a way his fellow Cubs fan would not be; his actions would be being shaped by his recent experience—a phenomenon known as the "ideomotor effect" (i.e., an idea-driven action: *ideo*/idea + *motor*/action).

How is all this relevant to SRM? Simple. If you hope to sell someone a product, service or experience, your chances of doing so increase dramatically if you take the consumers on a journey—or involve them in a story—*before* you make your pitch. That's precisely what SRM seeks to accomplish: first you engage with the consumer on a personal level, you establish a trusting two-way relationship—and (as in my previous example) only *then* do you propose your trip to Barcelona, or ask to get married. Traditional marketing cuts straight to the sale; in SRM, the relationship *always* comes first. And while the latter approach begins more slowly, the end result is not only more aesthetically and

---

[82] Daniel Kahneman, *Thinking, Fast and Slow* (New York: Farrar, Straus, and Giroux, 2011)

ethically satisfying, it's also more profitable, because you're laying the foundation for a long-term series of purchases rather than swooping in for a quick win.

Moreover, the SRM approach gets more productive over time because with every encounter, the seller knows the individual consumer better and better. The second law of thermodynamics says that everything in the universe steadily runs down and decays. But SRM defies that law. It gets more robust as information accumulates. It learns how many baseball tickets you like to buy, and how much you want to pay, and where you like to sit. So your offerings are progressively tailored to your desires and preferences.

Which companies are doing this well? Which can offer a model for ways to run your own company? Though every business will be a bit different. Let's look at a few businesses that are paving the way.[83]

By forming a partnership with Vivid Seats, ESPN demonstrated that it understands the priming model. Their sports highlights get fans in the ticket-buying mood, and then they provide a frictionless link to Vivid Seats—and walk away with a piece of every purchase. Brilliant. And everyone benefits: consumers, ESPN, and Vivid Seats.

As for establishing an emotional bond with consumers, consider Cisco. In 2016, the company launched a brand campaign called "There's Never Been a Better Time." Each one-minute video completed the sentence in a different way—some profound, some merely entertaining, e.g., "to connect those in need," "to change the world together," "to be an NBA fan." The company barely mentioned itself. Instead of focusing on the company's *products,* the videos focused on its *impacts.* Here's part of a typical script— pitched just right for Social Retail Marketing:

---

[83] Jordan Kasteler, "Eight Companies Doing Social Media Right and What Brands Can Learn from Them" (Social Media Marketing, marketingland.com, December 6, 2016)

Let's talk about now. Right now. Right now is happening so fast, you can barely keep up with it. Right now, we've got clouds protecting rhinos [image of drones hovering over several rhinos] and mobile technology finding clean water [image of a girl drinking from her cupped hands at a well in India]. Not tomorrow. Not five years in the future. Now. . . . And right now, this child [image of smiling boy in Africa] is being treated by a doctor from six-thousand miles away. This is science. Not fiction. . . . And there's never been a better time to change the world.

Will Elliott, the (now former) creative director of the ad agency Goodby Silverstein & Partners—describes the Cisco SRM approach (although they didn't call it SRM in 2016):

We did something kind of unusual for creatives. Cisco had a whole bunch of whitepapers, and we read them. We found out that Cisco technology is doing incredible things, amazing things. Suddenly we thought, "Oh my God. This stuff is so interesting." For example, Cisco technology allowed people to open a mobile bank in Zambia and Zaire—places where the regular banking system, and even the governments, aren't very stable. No one really knew where to keep their money, and now ordinary people can use their phones to store their money and buy things. It becomes this huge technological transformation.[84]

---

[84] Will Zanger, "'There's never been a better time': Cisco and GSP get optimistic in new work featuring Ewan McGregor" (thedrum.com, June 17, 2016)

By keeping the company in the background (sometimes referred to as "light branding"), Elliott focused on *technology* as a dramatic force for good, a more nuanced—and thus more believable—message than an obviously self-serving assertion that the *company* is a source of good. To be sure, each video ends with a quiet, almost whispered few seconds modestly suggesting, *Oh by the way, not that it's important, and we don't want to brag, but did we happen to mention that Cisco is the source of these technologies?* But by that point, the consumer has already viewed fifty-five seconds of breathtaking video and doesn't resent the closing reference. And by using the same opening line and the same cinematic style in each video, the company established a familiar template, one that viewers would instantly connect with other videos in the series. By resisting the urge to promote itself, Cisco did a better job of . . . promoting itself. And the company built a trusting relationship with consumers, one that will eventually pay bigger dividends than the traditional hard sell.

Rule Four: Offer Consumers Value and Purpose, and They Will Happily Allow You to Harness Their Profiles and Data

While Rule Three focuses on establishing a relationship with consumers, Rule Four concerns the *purpose* of that relationship and the *value* it adds to the consumer's life. This aligns with what former Google design ethicist Tristan Harris calls "time well spent," the idea that consumers should be able to look back on their social media experiences with a sense of accomplishment and a feeling that they are better off as a result of their exchanges. They are without regret that they'd have been better off doing something else.[85] To do that, sellers need to put

---

[85] Reem Najjar, "Could new design standards enhance positive time-spent with technology?" *UX Collective*, March 27, 2020 (https://uxdesign.cc/could-new-design-standards-enhance-positive-time-spent-with-technology-8994541b58cf)

themselves in the consumers' shoes, empathize with them, and answer these questions:

- Why should they want to interact with me rather than someone else?
- What unique benefits am I prepared to offer?
- Why should they give me access to their personal information?
- What's in it for them?

And the answers had better be larger than "Because I want to sell them something." If you aren't contributing to their well-being, if you aren't offering them relevant goods and services in a way other businesses can't, then your relationship is pointless, exploitive, and insincere. And modern consumers can sense insincerity in levels as low as one part per million. You can't fake sincerity. Not if you want your business to thrive.

If you're obliviously offering mixed martial arts tickets to a noncombative, sports-hating opera fan, if you're offering steakhouse coupons to a vegetarian, you aren't relevant, you aren't establishing a genuine community, and you have no purpose. You need to be clear about what you're offering in terms of time saved, costs cut, aggravation avoided, and opportunities expanded. *Consumers have a lot of choices.* You need to be clear about why they should choose you. You need to be clear that if they share their personal information, you'll reward them with the same kind of curated information they'd expect from a friend.

So let's imagine two marketers—SRM and Status Quo—are each developing their own social media community of art lovers to whom they hope to market products. Status Quo is on Facebook; SRM is on Instagram. As a potential customer, you're kind of uncommitted, on the fringes of both groups, but not really ensconced in either. You're making up your mind. And now there's an Escher exhibit at the Metropolitan Museum of Art. You know a little about Escher, but when you see the exhibit, you're awestruck, absolutely floored. You stare at his strange, compulsive, geometrically impossible lithographs and lose all sense of time. Suddenly, you realize you need to get back to the office, or you'll be late for a meeting.

But you've become so enthralled that you really want a copy of the exhibit catalog and an Escher biography. You glance at your Facebook feed, and Status Quo informs you that both are for sale in the museum's bookshop. But you see there's a fifteen-minute line at the store, and you came to the museum to look at Escher, not the back of a stranger's head. Now you really want the books. You want to read them tonight when you get home. The bookstore wants to sell books, and you want to buy them. But you can't connect. Unlike ESPN and Vivid Seats, Status Quo and you are in a lose-lose situation. You're primed to dislike the company. Your ideomotor indicator has entered the danger zone. Your lifestyle is not being enhanced. Your mind is not at rest.

Then you switch over to your Instagram feed and see that SRM offers both books and a BUY button, which 13 percent of consumers say would increase their likelihood of making a purchase.[86] You press it on your way out the door, knowing that both books will be on your porch when you get home. Your peace of mind returns. You're going to see the catalog and learn about the artist while your interest is at a fever pitch. As you're riding home in an Uber, you make a decision. SRM has provided value, and Status Quo has provided anti-value. So SRM gets your personal data, and Status Quo doesn't. And with the push of one more button, you withhold your digital identity from Status Quo.

---

[86] Paige Cooper, "43 Media Advertising Statistics That Matter to Marketers in 2020," bloghootsuite.com, April 23, 2020.

Rule Five: Invest in New Digital Channels and Technology So Consumers Can Control What, Where, When, and How They Consume

If you want to reap the benefits from SRM, you have to invest in it. That means allocating funds in your marketing budget and hiring marketers, designers, and copywriters who understand the medium, who know how to create in the new short formats and storytelling formats that social media demands. You can't just transfer your traditional marketing campaigns to SRM. That will do more harm than good.

Failing to fully embrace the new medium is one reason so many educational technologies have failed: too often developers just put their textbooks online. What's the point of that? It's like someone buying a Model T in 1912 and then hitching it to a team of horses. You need to take advantage of the power the new medium provides. A textbook can only present static images of an eclipse. But an interactive computer lesson can give students the power to manipulate the sun, earth, and moon. That produces a far richer experience. And the student learns more. But due to lack of imagination, fear of change, and the gravitational pull of old habits (as well as pure laziness), few educators have harnessed the new powers at their disposal.

Many marketers make the same mistake. Even those who redesign their old ads for social media tend to do this generically. They don't go far enough. They don't customize. They don't recognize that every platform offers different opportunities and constraints. You can't just transfer your image-centered Instagram campaign to a video channel, such as YouTube. What works on Facebook isn't going to work on Snapchat any more than a radio program would work on TV. Companies hoping to make SRM work need staff, specialists, and tools capable of exploiting the possibilities of each platform. Going halfway won't cut it. You're wasting time and money. You're like someone sitting in front of a TV with the sound off, unaware that the thing has a volume button.

The US food chain Chipotle has found that button. They're ahead of the curve and offer an example many companies should learn from. In June 2020, they did what I've been encouraging throughout the book: they stopped forcing you to open their app to place an order. Instead, you can do it from inside a social media feed—in this case, Facebook Messenger. You can keep chatting with your friends and, without leaving Messenger, order your dinner by silently interacting with their helpful bot (Pepper). Curt Garner, the company's CTO, explains that his goal is to meet customers where they hang out, which is on social media, not Chipotle's app:

> We're always working to enhance and optimize our digital capabilities and provide guests with a seamless ordering experience. It is critical that we meet customers where they are spending time online and give guests ordering options that best fit their needs.[87]

Many companies have made the shift to digital, but inexplicably ignore the vast potential of SRM. In the US, social media ad spending in 2020 ($43 billion) is just 32.8 percent of all digital advertising ($136 billion). The worldwide ratio is even lower: social media ad spending ($98.9 billion) is 29 percent of all digital advertising ($336 billion).[88] Shifting to digital and ignoring social is like driving from West Virginia

---

[87] Lucas Manfredi, "Chipotle enables ordering with Facebook Messenger thanks to new bot" (foxbusiness.com, June 18, 2020)

[88] Compiled from three sources: Sarah Cavil, "Digital Ad Spending Will Reach New Heights in 2020," insights.digital mediasolutions.com, January 10, 2020; Paige Cooper, "43 Social Media Advertising Statistics That Matter in 2020," (blog. hootsuite.com, April 23, 2020); Social Media Advertising (Statistica.com)

to Lake Ontario so you can fish for salmon and lake trout, and somehow ending up in a disconnected overflow pond full of nothing but sunfish and perch. You make the journey and have nothing to show for it.

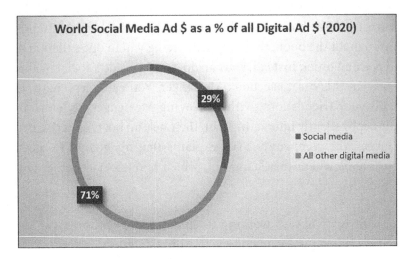

Most perplexing to me are the major insurance companies. The top property casualty firms spend $6.7 billion per year on ads, but as of October 2020, they have no social media presence. That's shocking! Especially since their business model is a perfect fit for SRM: they deliver instant, terse, personalized policy quotes. Yet they ignore the channels best suited to deliver these messages. Mind-boggling. You don't expect such reckless behavior from an insurance company.

They aren't following my rules. That has to change.

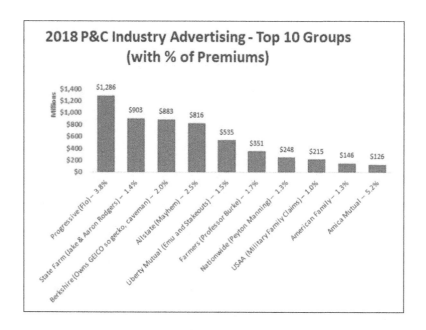

2018 P&C Industry Advertising - Top 10 Groups (with % of Premiums)

In the next chapter, we'll look at how the synergistic power of 5G mobile (i.e., the "fifth-generation" mobile network), AI, and social media as a distribution channel will hand the consumer new economic power. Although not all the buyers and sellers in the digital ecosystem see it yet, we are at an unprecedented period of development and opportunity due to interacting technological advancements in telecommunications, social networks, virtual and augmented reality, hardware, software, 3D printing, and distribution. In the next five years, the telecommunications industry will invest $1 trillion in 5G infrastructure, enabling better business models, novel concepts in education and entertainment, and improved digital financial, medical, and government services.

CHAPTER SEVEN

The Convergence: Selling in the Age of 5G Mobile, AI, and Social Media

A New Reality

WE'RE LIVING THROUGH AN UNPRECEDENTED PERIOD of development and opportunity due to synergistic technological advancements in mobile communications, social networks, AI, hardware, software, and distribution channels. The post-pandemic landscape will be exciting and challenging because our path has begun to steepen at an exponential rate as opposed to a linear one. New tactics and great resolve will be required to summit this slope. Although not all the players in the digital ecosystem can see where the path is leading, businesses need to prepare for a new reality in which consumers have greater and greater economic power. The convergence of 5G mobile connectivity, artificial intelligence (AI), and social media platforms is the foundation for creating SRM. In this environment, traditional marketing practices will flounder. Sellers who fail to adjust will weaken and collapse. In what follows,

I'll illuminate the way forward and help you turn the disruptions to your advantage so you can have a view from the mountaintop.

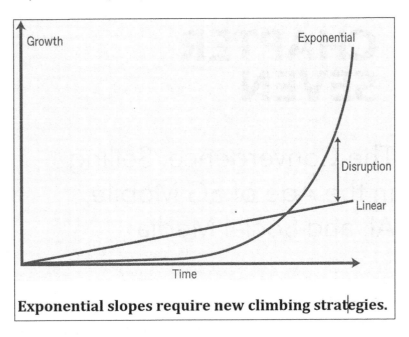

Exponential slopes require new climbing strategies.

What Is 5G Mobile?

In the next five years, the telecommunications industry will invest $1 trillion in 5G mobile infrastructure, enabling better business models, novel concepts in education and entertainment, and improved digital financial, medical, and government services. A brief history of the progression from 0G to 5G will clarify my optimism.

As Matt Bartlett notes, a network "generation" generally refers to a change in the fundamental nature of the service— non-backward-compatible transmission technology, higher peak bit rates, new frequency bands, wider channel frequency bandwidth in hertz, and higher capacity for many simultaneous data transfers."[89]

- "0G" refers to pre-cellular mobile phones, such as the radio systems used in cars. They became available after WWII.
- 1G systems were introduced in 1979. Like 0G, they were analog rather than digital. As boxy-looking as walkie-talkies, they transmitted at speeds of 2.4 kilobytes per second (Kbps). Just as older civilizations did not refer to themselves as "BC" or "BCE," the terms "0G" and "1G" were not coined until the advent of 2G technologies.
- 2G technology appeared in 1991 and enabled the first digitally encrypted phones. Transmission speeds increased by 500 percent to 14.4 Kbps.
- 3G technology increased transmission speeds by 900 percent to over 144 Kbps. Introduced in 1998, they enabled mobile internet access, fixed wireless access, and video calls.
- 4G networks, which have driven our modern smartphones, were introduced in Scandinavia in 2009, and the US in 2011. Transmission speeds were twenty times faster than 3G, enabling the host of options to which we have grown accustomed (e.g., making and playing videos).

With processing speeds one hundred times faster than 4G, the new 5G networks will deliver computing rates equivalent to—and soon greater than—the human brain, about 10^{16} cycles per second.[90] They are exponentially increasing connections among consumers, machines, and industries. 5G will ultimately allow

[89] Matt Bartlett, "The Evolution of Mobile Wireless Technology from 0G to 5G," *Medium*, November 26, 2019
[90] Peter H. Diamandis and Steven Kotler, *The Future Is Faster Than You Think* (New York: Simon and Schuster, 2020)

real-time virtual consumer experiences, limited only by imagination, inventiveness, and consumer desires. When AI, machine learning, and personalization algorithms are added to the mixture, automation and robotization will skyrocket, ultimately resulting in major enhancements in productivity, lifestyle, and well-being. These advances will nurture and deliver "killer" consumer experiences that will drive significant economic and societal benefits.

The Coming Explosion

Adoption rates for 5G increased 600 percent from 2019 to 2020; that's a miniscule jump compared to what's coming. From 2020 to 2023, that growth rate is expected to increase 1,376 percent, and by 2025, the number will be 2,817 percent. In other words, the 84 million current subscribers will rise to 2.4 billion in the next five years.

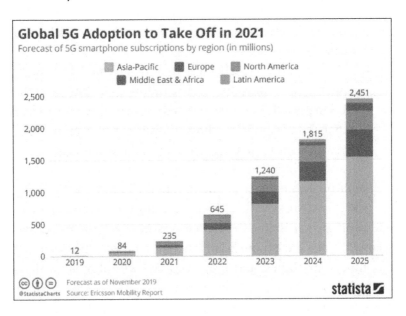

The Asia-Pacific region will account for the largest number of new adopters, but North America and Europe will also see staggering growth. Although Africa, the Middle East, and Latin America lag a bit behind, each will gain traction during this period, setting the stage for enormous increases later in the decade.

Global revenue generated by 5G wireless network infrastructure increased by $4.1 billion by the end of 2020, nearly double the 2019 number. And 5G's share of overall revenue is increasing at an astronomical rate. As 4G revenue falls by $4.1 billion from 2018 to 2021, revenue for 5G will increase by $6.7 billion, a difference of $10.8 billion.

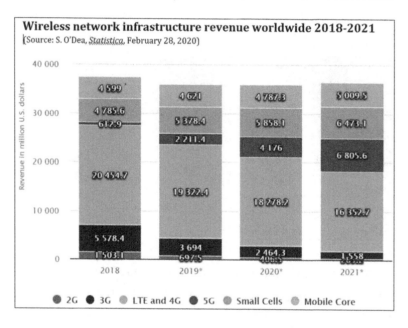

Wireless network infrastructure revenue worldwide 2018-2021
(Source: S. O'Dea, *Statistica*, February 28, 2020)

Moreover, a study by Juniper Research projects that 5G operator revenue will jump from $5 billion in 2020 to $357 billion by 2025—an increase of an astounding 7,040 percent.[91]

According to Katharina Buchholz, thirty-eight countries had already launched 5G networks by August 2020, and many more have begun to deploy them. In the next three years, 5G is expected to reach one billion users. As the map below shows, North

---

[91] "Operator Market Strategies: Challenges, Opportunities & Forecasts 2020–2025," Juniper Research, October 16, 2020

America, Europe, and East Asia lead the way. But almost every country in South America and South and Southeast Asia has partially deployed 5G mobile networks. In 3.5 years, such networks will likely reach an additional one billion users. South Korea had the first 5G network, and it's expected to stay in the lead for overall penetration. Within five years, 60 percent of the country's mobile subscriptions are expected to be for 5G networks.

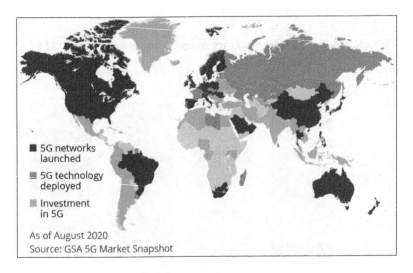

■ 5G networks launched
■ 5G technology deployed
■ Investment in 5G

As of August 2020
Source: GSA 5G Market Snapshot

As Diamandis and Kotler assert, we're fast approaching the time when "anyone who wants to be connected will be connected. . . . And as the population online *doubles*, we're likely to witness one of the most historic accelerations of technological innovation and global economic progress yet seen."[92] *Faster, wider,* and *better*—they're the watchwords of The Impatience Economy.

---

[92] Peter H. Diamandis and Steven Kotler, *Abundance: The Future Is Better than You Think*, (New York: Simon and Shuster, 2014).

Artificial Intelligence and Virtual Reality

The graph of transmission speeds from 1G to 5G networks closely resembles a right angle. It's as if we were walking along a slightly inclining sidewalk and then suddenly confronted the sheer vertical face of the Empire State Building. In some areas of our lives, this shift won't have much impact. Will you feel newly empowered if your texts arrive a nanosecond faster than they do now? Will you be ecstatic if the wait time required to download a movie decreases from two minutes to less than the time it takes to read the final five words of this sentence? Probably not—although in the Age of Impatience, who can say for sure?

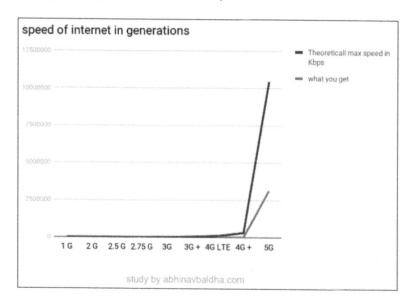

In other domains, however, the transformative shift is impossible to overstate. Consider AI and VR. Both have been around for decades, but for most of us, they were the equivalent of canned food to a man on a desert island with no can opener: Their potential calories were never going to reach his stomach. Rapid 5G networks are the equivalent of the missing opener—unlocking dormant possibilities in life-altering ways.

Suddenly, tools that have been restricted to tech giants will be available to consumers and SMEs. This is already happening. And it's a tremendous democratizing force that will increase competition and drive The Impatience Economy. Think of it: anyone with a 5G connection—which will soon be everyone—will have the real-time capability to have virtual experiences anywhere, anytime, without needing a landline, an internet connection, Wi-Fi, or the torturous-looking gear you'd expect to see on a diver about to be lowered into the Mariana Trench. As soon as your smartphone comes with a pair of unobtrusive glasses—and that's about to happen—we'll go through a society-wide step change on par with the invention of electricity.[93]

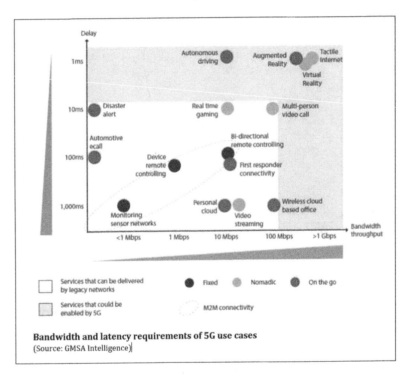

Bandwidth and latency requirements of 5G use cases
(Source: GMSA Intelligence)

[93] "How 5G Technology Will Affect Social Media" (https://www.brandinglosangeles.com/how-will-5g-technology-affect-social-media)

With 5G's extremely low latency (i.e., delay or lag time), immersive virtual or augmented experiences will be frictionless and lifelike—akin to the transition from the herky-jerky movements in early silent movies to the realistic sensation delivered by the modern standard of twenty-four frames per second. That's the difference between an enjoyable (and potentially life-altering) experience and a sickening one: most people feel nauseated with a delay of more than twenty milliseconds in a video feed. 4G typically produces fifty milliseconds of latency, so viewers are uncomfortable—like someone on a Tilt-A-Whirl. By contrast, 5G promises less than one millisecond of latency. With that performance, technologies will be processing images as fast or faster than the human brain. When Diamandis and Kotler published *The Future Is Faster Than You Think,* they meant, "faster than you *realize.*" But their title is unintentionally true in a literal way: the new technologies are going to outpace the speed of thought. Virtual experiences can provide consumers with some immediate benefits. Before you go on vacation, why not walk around the streets of a few cities to see which one you like best? Before you swipe the buy bar on your mobile phone to buy a suit or a pair of shoes, why not try them on—wherever you happen to be—so you can determine if they look as good on you as they do on the model? Before you risk seasickness on that cruise you've wanted to take, why not slip on a headset and take a test trip you can terminate at the first sign of queasiness? In all these cases, buyer's remorse will become a thing of the past.

And the cost of VR experiences has dropped precipitously. As VR pioneer Jeremy Bailenson told an audience at NYU's School of Law, in 2015, a pair of quality VR goggles would set you back $40,000—more than many consumers were willing (or able) to pay for a car; at the time, there were fewer than two thousand pairs in existence.[94] Today, you can get a serviceable hookup for the price of a decent bottle of wine, and there are more than fifteen million owners in the US alone.

Walk a Mile in My Shoes

Social media is often seen as a divisive force, bringing out the worst in us, increasing tribalism, and accelerating our contempt for one another. The University of Maryland's Nathan Jurgenson, for example, sees social media as driving "the growing atmosphere of dissent that is enveloping much of the globe" and creating a "flammable atmosphere" of rioting and violence.[95] At the other extreme are authors like Neil Postman, who trivialize social media activity as way of "amusing ourselves to death." Indeed, an entire subgenre of bestselling books—such as Nicholas Carr's Pulitzer Prize–nominated *The Shallows: What the Internet Is Doing to Our Brains*—lament (paradoxically) our current twitchy inability to read the very books we are reading. We're told that social media will degrade our personal relationships and that AI will soon enslave us through the exertion of what philosopher Nick Bostrom calls a "superintelligence," over which we will inevitably lose control. One day, IBM supercomputer Deep Blue beats Garry Kasparov at chess; the next, we're a herd of cows providing milk for our silicon overlords.

Clearly, a wise society casts a cold eye on any potential danger to its foundational beliefs. Hector and his minions needed a better surveillance program the day they opened their gates and accepted the Trojan horse. Too late, they learned to "Beware of Greeks bearing gifts." But the moral of that story is not "Never

---

[94] See Bailenson's 2019 NYU lecture (https://vhil.stanford.edu/video/2019/jeremy-bailenson-the-virtues-of-virtual-reality/#more-8335)
[95] Nathan Jurgenson, "When Atoms Meet Bits: Social Media, The Mobile Web, and Augmented Revolution," (Future Internet, January 23, 2012)

accept a gift." There's such a thing as protecting oneself to death. As Ronald Reagan said, "Trust, but verify."

What is often overlooked by these dystopians is that immersive experiences can also produce large-scale social benefits in ways that were previously unimaginable. VR is already providing exposure-therapy benefits to Iraq war veterans suffering from post-traumatic stress disorder.[96] It's also proving legal benefits to crime victims. "There are incredible possibilities to using this technology in the court system," attorney Noel Edin tells Bloomberg Law. VR could be used to "transport a jury to the intersection where an accident occurred or to a grisly crime scene. Rather than *hearing* about a car crash, juries can *experience* that crash. I believe, in ten years, most lawyers will be using VR the way they use laptops today."[97]

Want to know what a police officer sees and feels when he confronts a knife-wielding assailant? Juries can now have that experience. The same holds for those nonprofit businesses trying to raise awareness about people with disabilities or impoverished children in Calcutta. It's one thing to read a story and *try* to make an imaginative leap to another person's plight; it's another to *inhabit* that person's body and *experience* her travails.

In his lecture called The Virtues of Virtual Reality: How Immersive Technology Can Reduce Bias, Jeremy Bailenson says that when one takes on an avatar, he implicitly *becomes* that avatar.[98] It takes about four minutes. At that point, the subject looking into a virtual mirror identifies with the VR image rather

---

[96] Albert A. Rizzo, JoAnn Difede, B.O. Rothnaum, Scott Johnston, Robert N. McLay, Greg Reiger, Greg Gahm, Thomas Parsons, Ken Graap, and Jarrell Pair, "VR PTSD Exposure Therapy Results with Active Duty OIF/OEF Combatants" (*Medicine Meets Virtual Reality* 17, IOS Press, 2009)

[97] Sara E. Teller, "The Use of Virtual Reality in the Courtroom," *Legal Reader: News and Politics*, November 21, 2017 (https://www.legalreader.com/use-virtual-reality-courtroom/)

[98] Jeremy Bailenson, *Experience on Demand: What Virtual Reality Is, How It Works, and What It Can Do* (New York: W.W. Norton, 2018)

than her embodied self. An Irish woman in Dublin *is* a child in Calcutta. "As far as your brain is concerned," Bailenson says, "that experience isn't virtual; it's real." In essence, VR becomes an empathy machine. Those who see immersive experiences as a self-absorbed, escapist hobby for the privileged, should reconsider the social costs of their easy dismissal, their inability to fully imagine the social benefits of the new technology. Just as VR can allow consumers to see themselves in tuxedos and wedding dresses, it can also allow us to see ourselves with one another. As 5G prepares to invite 4.2 billion new voices into the global conversation, that ability will add to our collective well-being. VR will contribute to the rapid growth of SRM by giving consumers informative sensory experiences when discovering, buying, and consuming goods and services.

Access to AI: Plug and Play

AI has never been as accessible as it is now—through the most basic type of subscription service. Both Google and Facebook offer AI platforms. So does IBM Watson. These are straightforward, plug-and-play options. So companies don't have to hire specialists and develop their own systems. They don't have to reinvent that very expensive wheel. Instead, they just pay a nominal access fee. That eliminates a huge barrier to development. In the past, industries have tended to focus (improvidently) on themselves, failing to see how they could leverage other advancements, technologies, access, and distribution points. They've worked in a vertical manner, trying to do it all themselves. That's not sustainable; you don't save money by sewing your own clothes. You've more productive ways to spend your time. A company selling travel services shouldn't build its own AI any more than Ford should make its own tires.

Not everyone within each industry and sector fully appreciates the power of the 5G-AI convergence, but the wiser ones are starting to. It's not something new; it's just new to them. Google, Facebook, and Amazon have been using AI for years. They've built their businesses by combining their access to consumers with precise analytics—and then using that information to provide valuable products and services. With the advent of plug-and-play AI, SMEs can now follow this same model. We're about to see a revolutionary scaling effect.

Some SMEs used to think that AI was hype—or perhaps that attitude was just sour grapes because they couldn't afford it—but Google, Facebook, and Amazon have proven how powerful and essential it is to understanding and reaching consumers. What looked like science fiction is now accepted reality. You simply can't survive unless you can process a tremendous amount of data on user behavior and develop actionable insights grounded in that behavior. AI offers an unparalleled ability to identify hidden links and patterns in what looks—to the most discerning human eye—like a pile of random nonsense.

Even though Garry Kasparov beat Deep Blue, the time will come when even the best chess player in the world has zero chance of beating an AI-powered opponent, which—because of machine learning—has been steadily improving its performance in a way that the human brain cannot. When a company employing AI competes with one that eschews it, the result is equally one-sided—and the gap between the two widens every minute as more data accumulates. When it's man versus machine, don't be sentimental: bet on the machine.

We're all interacting with AI all the time, whether we know it or not. Every time you do a search, Google or Amazon refines your profile so they can make more accurate predictions about other products and services that might interest you. Natural language processing is becoming so effective, consumers will soon be unable to tell whether they are talking to a person or a bot. Diamandis and Kotler report that the Tel Aviv start-up Beyond Verbal has built an AI-driven customer service coach that can reliably identify four hundred different markers of your mood and personality to tell what kind of consumer you are. If you're an early adopter, for example, the system alerts the sales staff to offer you one set of purchasing options; if you sound reluctant, you'll get a different pitch. This is emotionally intelligent computing that promotes quick, frictionless shopping. Good luck finding a similarly astute employee from ZipRecruiter. And Beyond Verbal doesn't eat lunch, grow tired in the afternoon, or get distracted by watching TikTok or checking their Robinhood stock portfolios.

Until recently, however, these kinds of tools have been simply too complex for most small and medium-sized businesses to employ. They lack the skilled personnel to make them work. When International Data Corporation surveyed 2,473 companies around the globe, they found that most AI efforts had failed. But the *Wall Street Journal* says that offerings like Amazon Kendra and Contact Lens, both released in 2019, are changing that:

> "There's no machine-learning expertise required for either of these services. They're just plug and play. You don't have to get into all the weeds and get the training data and label the data and all those sorts of things," said Matt Wood, vice president for artificial intelligence services at Amazon Web Services. "You're getting better visibility; it's bringing into focus the interactions your customers are having with your organization, day by day, minute by minute, and allowing you to inspect that on a level that just wasn't possible before."[99]

And because your smartphone now has so much computing

---

[99] Agam Seth, "Amazon Introduces 'Plug and Play AI Tools," *The Wall Street Journal*, December 23, 2019.

power, you can do all this without being tethered to your desk or your laptop.

Spend Smart: Apps versus Bots

As we saw in Chapter 5, developing a quality app can cost $70,000 to $100,000.[100] That's a prohibitive investment for many small businesses. And as I've emphasized, it's also a backward-looking approach, given consumers' growing resistance to apps. Just as you didn't want to be the last person to pay $7,999 for an eighty-inch LED screen, neither do you want to be the last person to invest a fortune, particularly in an app no one downloads or uses.

Fortunately, you have cheaper and more promising options. For less than $200 you can get a bot or chatbot (e.g., Chatfuel) that will put you inside consumers' social media feeds—precisely where you want to be. On its own, however, that bot is rather limited. It's not Alexa or Siri. It gives preprogrammed answers and is pretty clunky. But it's a foot in the door.

So then you use Facebook Chat Plugin, which integrates a Messenger experience directly into your company website and lets you communicate with and respond to customers with greater fluency. Now you're leveraging Facebook's AI, machine learning, natural language processing, and voice recognition. Maybe you use IBM's Watson to process a lot of the data. For an extra $59.99 a month, you can process your payments.

Keep in mind that you aren't building any of this. You're simply putting together a menu of plug-and-play options. And even to-day—before economies of scale and competition lower the prices—you can get this kind of functionality to converse with consumers and sell products for $7,000 to $10,000. And the technology is only going to get better, faster, and cheaper. So you're saving $90,000,

---

[100] "How Much Does It Cost to Make An App?" (https://www.goodfirms.co/resources/mobile-app-development-cost)

and you're better positioned to make sales than the guy with the fancy app no one wants now, let alone two years from now.

I won't use this book for promoting my company FastForward.ai | The Social Retail Marketing Platform™, but I will say that companies like FastForward.ai and others that will certainly follow are capable of providing turnkey solutions to offer large and small medium-sized enterprises to reach, sell, and serve customers across all the top social media and messaging channels with a single point of integration and management. Companies can easily and quickly have a platform that would cost tens or hundreds of millions of dollars if developed by a large enterprise, for a modest monthly subscription cost.

CEOs face a lot of hard choices, but this isn't one of them.

More Convergence: Drones, 3D Printing, and Customized Products

I would need another book to discuss all the implications of the 5G-AI-SRM convergence, but before I close, let me highlight few more tools of particular relevance to business leaders.

Drones. In The Impatience Economy, delivery speed becomes more and more vital. You may think drones are confined to military use and have nothing to do with your company. You'd better hope your competitors are similarly deluded. Drone use is (literally) skyrocketing. Powered by 5G networks, drones will become faster, safer, and more accurate. Commercial drone revenues increased from $0.6 billion in 2014 to $2.4 billion in 2020; by 2024, the number will be $12.6 billion. Drone deliveries will account for, by far, the largest fraction of that growth.[101] In 2016, there were 110,000 drones in the sky; by 2024, there will be 2.6 million.

---

[101] "The Drone Delivery Market, Forecast to 2024," *Research and Markets*, March 25, 2020

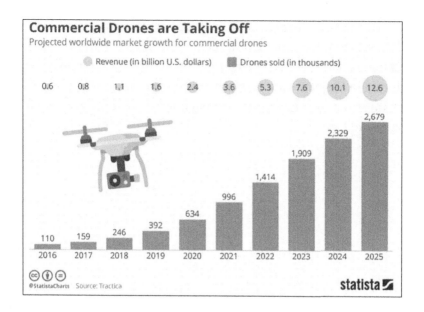

Commercial Drones are Taking Off
Projected worldwide market growth for commercial drones

Revenue (in billion U.S. dollars)   Drones sold (in thousands)

| 0.6 | 0.8 | 1.1 | 1.6 | 2.4 | 3.6 | 5.3 | 7.6 | 10.1 | 12.6 |

2016	2017	2018	2019	2020	2021	2022	2023	2024	2025
110	159	246	392	634	996	1,414	1,909	2,329	2,679

@StatistaCharts   Source: Tractica

statista

Customized products. Current 3D printers can produce every-thing from car parts to prosthetic limbs. Usage is going up, and prices are coming down. As a result, consumers will no longer have to settle for a "close-enough" product. Why buy a one-size-fits-all shoe when you can send a scan of your feet to a store that quickly prints you a custom-made pair to accommodate the precise curve of the fallen arch on your left foot and your slightly smaller right foot. This is the difference from selecting reading glasses from various preset magnifications in a drugstore bin and visiting an eye doctor who can account for the specific differences in each eye. Nike, Adidas, and other companies have already combined AI and 3D printing to produce personalized running shoes.[102] According to *Forbes,* revenues for the 3D industry are expected to climb from $15.8 billion in 2020 to $35.6 billion in 2024, an increase of 125 percent.[103]

---

[102] Carlotta V, "Why Combine Artificial Intelligence and 3D Printing," 3Dnatives. com, January 6, 2020.

[103] T.J. McHue, "Significant 3D Printing Forecast Surges To $35.6 Billion," Forbes, March 27, 2019.

In the next chapter, we'll look at how the analysis of large data sets with AI can help develop your business and improve customer satisfaction. With 60 zettabytes of data about to come online in the next two years, the need to translate that Niagara of information into powerful insights will be crucial to your survival.

CHAPTER EIGHT

Insights Trump Data

Data, Data Everywhere

UNDER THE HEADLINE "THE WORLD'S MOST VALUABLE Resource Is No Longer Oil, but Data," the May 2017 issue of *The Economist* featured a drawing of six offshore drilling platforms, each branded with a company logo: Amazon, Facebook, Google, Tesla, Uber, and Microsoft. The message was clear: data is the oil of the digital era.[104] Several months later, Ajay Banga, the president and CEO of MasterCard made the same point, telling a Saudi audience, "I believe that data is the new oil. I'm saying it in this country because I believe that the prosperity that oil brought in the last fifty years, data will bring in the next fifty, one hundred years if you use it the right way."[105]

Like most metaphors, however, the oil-as-data trope conceals as much as it reveals. Unlike data, oil is a finite resource. You pump it for keeps. We may develop more innovative and efficient

---

[104] "Regulating the Data Economy: The World's Most Valuable Resource," *The Economist*, May 6, 2017

[105] David Reid, Mastercard's Boss Just Told a Saudi Arabian Audience That 'Oil Is the New Data,'" cnbc.com, October 24, 2017

extraction methods, but at some point, the supply will dry up. Not so with data; the nonpolluting, reusable supply has been steadily doubling every three years since 2000—with no end in sight.

Our language struggles to keep pace with this escalation. Terms like "gigabyte" and "megabyte" (a one followed by six zeros) have been superseded by "zettabyte" (a one followed by twenty-one zeros). From 2020 to 2025, the global datasphere is expected to grow by over 190 percent, from about sixty to over 175 zettabytes. The scale of this nonlinear increase is almost impossible to fathom. As the physicist Albert Bartlett famously pointed out, "The greatest shortcoming of the human race is our inability to understand the exponential function."[106] But Adam Schlosser of the World Economic Forum offers some sense of what those numbers mean in human terms: forty zettabytes is "roughly equivalent to four million years of HD video or five billion Libraries of Congress." Researchers at Purdue University offer an equally stunning analogy: a megabyte is a short novel, a gigabyte is Beethoven's Fifth Symphony, and a zettabyte is "as much information as there are grains of sand on all the world's beaches."[107] Multiply those grains by 115, and you'll have a dizzying sense of how much data we will add in the next five years.

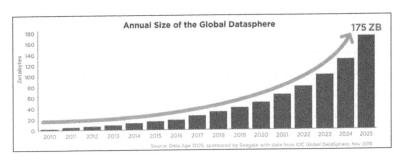

[106] Albert Bartlett, *The Essential Exponential* (Lincoln, Nebraska: The Center for Science, Mathematics, and Computer Education, 2004)
[107] "Information Technology: Rise of the Data Analyst—What's behind the Boom?" Purdue University Global, September 16, 2019 (https://www.purdueglobal.edu/blog/information-technology/rise-of-data-analyst/)

By itself, however, mere data is relatively worthless—like a library full of haphazardly arranged books written in a language you can't read. Data takes on value only when we convert it into *information* that leads to actionable insights. In this chapter, we'll look more deeply into the specifics of this conversion process—and at the new tools, services, and strategies that will enable your SRM efforts to transmute the lead of inert and unedifying data into the golden and melodious ringing of a cash register.

Signal and Noise

In information theory, "noise" is any input that distorts or corrupts the message (or "signal") between the sender and the receiver. Like static on a phone line, misspellings, or sloppy penmanship, noise can entirely obscure meaning or simply require more time to disentangle it. But in these cases, we have no difficulty identifying the two components: the noise is the crackling sound, and the signal is the human voice we struggle to hear.

Large data sets present another kind of problem. Unlike a radio broadcast, they aren't explicit attempts to convey meaning. A conglomeration of facts about cholesterol levels or the collective buying behavior of US consumers isn't trying to tell us something. The data may contain useful information, but it's up to us to extract it. In such cases, the signal and the noise are not clearly differentiated.

Because our minds are pattern-making machines, we are prone to making erroneous connections, to conflating signal and noise. If it's raining and I have a stomach ache, it's possible to make the false connection that rain causes stomach aches. If I look at shopping behavior and my data shows that Jane, John, Joan, and Jim all bought watches on a Wednesday, I might conclude that this is no coincidence: people whose first names begin with "J" love watches and always buy them on the third day of the week. If

I built my marketing strategy around this random coincidence, I'm mistaking noise for signal. Knowing the difference between signal and noise is the difference between astrology and astronomy, between pursuing real business opportunities and figments of the imagination, and ultimately between financial growth and bankruptcy.

For executives facing mountains of data with nothing but their biologically evolved mental hardware and software, the chance of their extracting reliable insights is about as likely as their winning the lottery. But the digital age has given us the potential to change that by augmenting our limited natural intelligence with superhuman calculating tools and AI. Some industries have overlooked that potential—to their detriment. Mobile operators have had reams of data for thirty years. They've known where we are and what we are doing, but they've never processed that data, turned it into information, and acted on it. No business that hopes to survive in The Impatience Economy can afford to repeat that mistake.

To thrive, companies must make decisions based on separating signals from noisy data—acting on facts, numbers, and patterns of consumer behavior rather than trusting their investment capital to the gut instincts of Mad Men marketing gurus. Failing to do this is a recipe for self-destruction—like spotting your competitors a ten-meter head start in a one-hundred-meter race or flying an airplane on a cloudy night "by the seat of your pants" rather than relying on your instruments. A pilot's natural instincts are not trustworthy, and neither are those of a CEO. Fortunately, data can serve as a kind of marketing altimeter. Every year, consumers leave a broader digital trace about their preferences and inclinations. Over the past five years, the number of data interactions per consumer per day jumped from 584 to 1,426—an increase of 144 percent. In the next five years, that number will increase by an additional 244 percent.

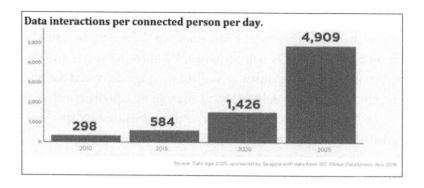

Data interactions per connected person per day.

4,909

1,426

584

298

| 2010 | 2015 | 2020 | 2025 |

Source: Data Age 2025, sponsored by Seagate with data from IDC Global DataSphere, Nov 2018

Businesses that interpret this data and extract insights to act upon it will be better able to target potential customers and deliver more contextually valuable products and services. Those that don't, will be doing the equivalent of flying with their eyes closed. The probability of an eventual crash is 100 percent.

In The Impatience Economy, consumers make quick purchasing decisions, so businesses need more than just a large *volume* of data to analyze—they also need *moment-by-moment updates* to that data. After all, the information that a consumer wants to buy a car has zero value once he makes the purchase. The window closed before you even knew it was open. A social media story that might have engaged and swayed the buyer during the shopping phase instantly becomes irrelevant and annoying once he drives off the dealership's lot. Buying a car is just not relevant to him anymore.

Fortunately for businesses, a rapidly growing fraction of the global datasphere is available in real time. After holding steady at about one zettabyte from 2010 to 2015, it jumped to ten zettabytes in 2020. But that's just the beginning. In the next five years, real-time data will increase by forty zettabytes (i.e., four million years of HD video or all the grains of sand on forty earths). In other words, the percentage of the world's data available in real time will have increased from less than 1 percent in 2010 to 30 percent in 2025. The speed with which businesses can process this data and engage users through their social media channels will determine who survives and who does not. Like a student sitting for an SAT test, CEOs will be judged by both the speed and the precision of their responses. A skillful message delivered too late or a clumsy message delivered on time will be equally fruitless.

As I wrote in previous chapters, those businesses who have invested the time and effort to establish trusted SRM relationships will be ideally positioned to act on real-time data. Starting from scratch at this point in the sales process inevitably looks old-school and transactional in a way that modern consumers won't tolerate. You're like the suitor who proposes marriage on the first date.

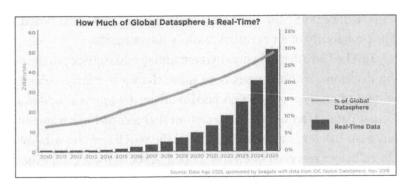

How Much of Global Datasphere is Real-Time?

Source: Data Age 2025, sponsored by Seagate with data from IDC Global DataSphere, Nov 2018

Democratizing Information: The Growth of Business Analytics

In previous chapters, I explained how SRM campaigns pay to use AI-driven tools provided by data giants like Facebook, Amazon, and Google. Doing so enables them to put their products in front of targeted audiences. The big change is coming, when more players will enter the marketplace and companies will have greater and more affordable access to the full range of analytic resources. These resources will allow them to process data from their own environment, their own customer base, their own target audience, their own websites, and their own apps. As a result, they'll be able to mine the kind of reliable insights that increase efficiency, customer satisfaction, and sales. The precondition for such progress is mass-market access to tools previously available only to the data giants.

One harbinger of this change is the explosive growth of new academic disciplines: business analytics, data science, and data analytics. Just as there was no need for microbiologists prior to the invention of the microscope, there was little need for data experts before the arrival of big data. And just as a layperson has zero chance of developing a COVID-19 vaccine by staring through a high-tech eyepiece, an old-school business owner has little chance of expanding and optimizing her business simply because she has access to an ocean of data or, as I mentioned before, because she just posts "digital billboards" on Facebook. In both cases, changes in technology demand new kinds of expertise and a different mindset.

Fortunately, help is on the way. Ten years ago, not a single US university offered an advanced degree in data analysis. Today, more than three hundred schools do so, turning out more than ten thousand graduates per year. And that number is sure to increase dramatically in foreseeable future. The first Master of Science in Analytics program was founded at North Carolina State University in 2007 with funds from the privately owned business analytics company SAS, in part to generate job applicants with the requisite skills to serve its clients. The school's founding document states the following: "As the need of analytics becomes more widespread, there is mounting demand for professionals with strong quantitative skills coupled with an understanding of how the techniques are applied to a variety of critical tasks facing decision-makers."[108]

---

[108] The Institute for Advanced Analytics, North Carolina State University, Michael Rappa, Goodnight Director and Distinguished Professor (https://analytics.ncsu.edu/reports/msa.pdf)

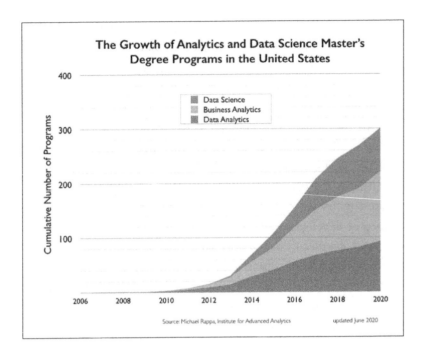

The Growth of Analytics and Data Science Master's Degree Programs in the United States

Source: Michael Rappa, Institute for Advanced Analytics   updated June 2020

The data analytics market is providing plenty of work for these new graduates—and not all of them will be working at today's handful of big data firms. From 2015 to 2019, the analytics market more than doubled in value, from $24 billion to $49 billion. From 2020 to 2023, the market's compound annual growth rate is expected to be over 30 percent—or $77.6 billion.[109] As competition increases, CEOs will have wider, cheaper, and better options than when they were forced to work exclusively with the tech giants. That's true whether they hire specialists to work directly for their companies or contract services from newly formed analytics businesses.

Palantir Technologies—co-founded by Peter Thiel—offers a good example of an analytics company that is broadening the

---

[109] Data Analytics Market in 2020: Trends, Forecasts, and Challenges, Cognetik, January 7, 2020 (https://www.cognetik.com/blog/data-analytics-market-in-2020-trends-forecasts-challenges/)

range of choices available to companies and CEOs. Named after the magical "seeing stones" that allow characters in J. R. R. Tolkien's *The Lord of the Rings* to see what would otherwise be hidden, Palantir is similarly magical in its ability to process data and reveal what would otherwise be unseen connections in consumer behavior across multiple platforms, sources, and formats—everything from archaic data to real time information—and then synthesize it, analyze it, and present it in a relational manner to enhance decision-making. Palantir's original clients were counterterrorism analysts in the US Intelligence Community and the Department of Defense. Its facial-recognition technology helps protect our airports, identify and track potentially malevolent actors, and so on. More recently, however, Palantir has begun to serve businesses by licensing analytic software as a *subscription service* rather than operating as a consulting company. Its acquisition of Kimono Labs has improved its ability to collect data from public-facing websites; its acquisition of the data-visualization start-up Silk enables it to deliver more easily accessible information.

Palantir recognizes that businesses often fail to fulfill their potential because their data is fragmented and locked in silos. As a result, frontline managers often lack crucial information when they need it most. Palantir helps businesses integrate disperse data onto one platform, empowering entire organizations to answer complex questions quickly by bringing the right information to the right people at the right time in formats they can readily understand and use.

Palantir is just one of many companies who are key enablers of the Second Consumer Revolution and will be key players in The Impatience Economy. Customer relationship management (CRM) efforts by Salesforce, HubSpot, NetSuite, and others are providing more and more sophisticated tools to manage large client bases. As businesses tailor these tools to their SRM efforts—which is starting to happen—the playing field will level off in a hurry.

Sooner rather than later, small and medium-sized businesses are going to have what the big players have already. We tend to think that the current power dynamics are durable. But that's not how life works. Dinosaurs go extinct. The Roman Empire falls. Buster Douglas knocks out Mike Tyson. The environment changes, and new champions emerge.

If a new brand or a smaller company offers something valuable to consumers, they're now able to discover it through SRM in a way they couldn't in the past. These new companies will grow through word of mouth. Consumers love to tell their social media friends about great new products, services, companies, or brands. And that can fuel exponential growth capable of displacing any company resting on its laurels. It seems unthinkable that big brands will disappear, but you can be 100 percent sure a number of them will. Marsupial wolves were an efficient and ferocious apex predator in Tasmania for thousands of years. They had huge crocodilian jaws. But when the more robust mastiffs showed up on European ships, those animals were doomed. In a generation, they were gone. Completely. Extinct. All that remains are their bones. It's the law of the jungle, and let's not kid ourselves, that same cruel rule governs the marketplace.

Look at what happened in the mobile phone space. Where's Motorola today? Gone. Where is Palm? Gone. These were multibillion-dollar companies, and in the span of a few years, they disappeared from the landscape because they didn't keep up with the change in consumer behavior and technology. The eerily steep graphs of these companies' decline mirror the path of the Niagara River when it reaches the deadly Horseshoe Falls and heads toward the inescapable vortex of the Niagara Whirlpool. They offer a cautionary tale to anyone who mistakes the status quo for a solid foundation. And those newcomers poised to exploit the full potential of SRM will be perfectly positioned to create and exploit the tectonic shift that is coming—the prime beneficiary of which will be the consumer.

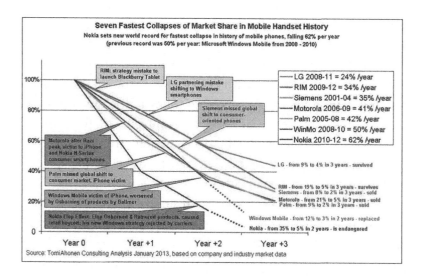

Seven Fastest Collapses of Market Share in Mobile Handset History
Nokia sets new world record for fastest collapse in history of mobile phones, falling 62% per year
(previous record was 50% per year: Microsoft Windows Mobile from 2008 - 2010)

LG 2008-11 = 24% /year
RIM 2009-12 = 34% /year
Siemens 2001-04 = 35% /year
Motorola 2006-09 = 41% /year
Palm 2005-08 = 42% /year
WinMo 2008-10 = 50% /year
Nokia 2010-12 = 62% /year

LG - from 9% to 4% in 3 years - survived
RIM - from 19% to 5% in 3 years - survives
Siemens - from 8% to 2% in 3 years - sold
Motorola - from 21% to 5% in 3 years - sold
Palm - from 9% to 2% in 3 years - sold
Windows Mobile - from 12% to 3% in 2 years - replaced
Nokia - from 35% to 5% in 2 years - is endangered

Source: TomiAhonen Consulting Analysis January 2013, based on company and industry market data

A Two-Sided Street

Thus far in this chapter, I've stressed the role of technology in converting raw data into actionable insights. But CEOs must recognize that the acquisition of new tools is a necessary, but not sufficient, condition for their businesses to thrive in The Impatience Economy. Owning a scientific calculator may be necessary to solve a complex physics problem, but in the hands of a typical college graduate, all those special function keys are useless. He has no idea what they mean. You might as well hand a trombone and some sheet music to a chimpanzee, and expect him to translate the notes into a jazz melody. It's not going to happen. Being a surgeon requires more than a scalpel.

To unlock the potential power of the new technologies, to convert mute data into lucrative insights, CEOs need to reconsider every aspect of their businesses. If tech advancements are one side of the street, new business paradigms about how to integrate those advancements into day-to-day managerial decisions are the other. Technology isn't a panacea. Business isn't a paint-by-numbers project. Real art is required. You don't just click a bunch of boxes and magically receive a formula to transform your company. You have to know what you are clicking, why you are clicking it, and what target audience you are seeking. You need to know how to ask the right questions, which is a new skill and far more challenging than it sounds. You need to know how to interpret the data and insights. At the end of the day, someone still has to make judgments—and they are qualitatively different from the kinds of judgments you've made in the past. AI can do part of that, but defining precisely where and how to apply AI is a complex decision that can mean the difference between success and failure.

To appreciate this challenge, let's compare the advent of these new technologies to another period of rapid change: the replacement of steam engines by electrical power.[110] Today, most of us assume this shift brought about a *rapid* increase in productivity. But that isn't true. Why? Because of what economists call the "productivity paradox" (also called the "Solow paradox"[111]). To simplify a bit, the central idea here is that the ultimate potential of a new idea tends to be hamstrung—sometimes for long intervals—by the hidebound ideas of early adopters, who lack the creativity or courage (or both) to shift their business paradigms in ways that optimize a new invention's power. It's as if someone who has always used a wheelbarrow were given a truck, which he then loads with cargo, shifts into neutral, and pushes around town to make his deliveries.

Something almost as absurd happened in the decades after Edison built the first electrically powered motor for factory use. As economists Erik Brynjolfsson and Andrew McAfee point out, most companies simply bought the largest electric motors they could afford "and stuck them unimaginatively where the steam engines used to be. . . . There may have been less smoke and a

---

[110] Tim Hartford, "Why Didn't Electricity Immediately Change Manufacturing?" BBC World Service, August 20, 2017 (https://www.bbc.com/news/business-40673694)
[111] Robert Solow, "We'd Better Watch Out," *The New York Times Book Review*, July 12, 1987

little less noise . . . but productivity barely budged. Only after thirty years—long enough for the original managers to retire and be replaced by a new generation—did factory layouts change." Instead of the single, *centralized* massive engine steam production required, these new managers reenvisioned the production process, opting for a *distributed* system in which "each piece of equipment had its own small electric motor. Instead of putting the machines needing the most power closest to power source, the improved layout was based on a simple and powerful new principle: the natural workflow of materials." At that point, "productivity didn't merely inch up on the resulting assembly lines; it doubled or even tripled."[112]

In the modern, hypercompetitive Impatience Economy, this kind of drawn-out adherence to the status quo spells doom. My aim in this book is to help you avoid that fate. Success will come only to those who understand how to think digital and how to dream digital—how to think social and dream social. CEOs must have the will to recreate all experiences from the ground up, asking themselves, "How do consumers behave inside social media?" rather than pledging allegiance to how they've always done marketing, which is just to bombard consumers with messages saying, "Like my products!" and waiting for them to come to them and buy.

Businesses will also need to transform their own internal divisions so that the marketing side and the retail sales side are more aligned—or even combined—rather than siloed. You won't survive if you have different decision-makers using separate metrics. You can't have compartmentalized departments working at cross purposes or executives congratulating themselves as they unwittingly negate each other's conflicting achievements. And you can't run an effective SRM program if

---

[112] Erik Brynjolfsson and Andrew McAfee, *The Second Machine Age: Work, Progress, and Prosperity in a Time of Brilliant Technologies* (New York: W.W. Norton and Company, 2015)

your customer service, sales, and marketing departments have conflicting visions. Three voices on a single social media channel? That can't help but create a sense of cognitive dissonance in your potential customers. Such dissonance discomfits buyers and destroys sales opportunities. Who trusts an incoherent company? Who has faith in its products or services? All the data management tools in the world can't overcome these mistakes. Don't neglect this side of the street. Technology alone can't solve these problems.

The Cost of Converting Data into Insights

Until recently, many businesses have had no easy or affordable way to make this conversion. But as subscription services of the sort now offered by Palantir, IBM's Watson, and others become available, more and more opportunities will be on the table. Companies that couldn't (or wouldn't) start their own analytics division can now outsource that work at reasonable prices—especially when CEOs consider the cost of *failing* to obtain this information (i.e., the scuttling of their entire business). A small enterprise can get a subscription for $5,000 to $10,000 a month—a large enterprise, for $15,000 to $25,000. At these rates, the benefits of being able to target a curated roster of consumers far outweigh the costs.

As of this writing, most companies still need several subscriptions, one doing the data and analytics, another doing the front-end interface with the consumer, and a third doing the back-end integration into their business systems. This was a key motivation and driver in my founding FastForward.ai | The Social Retail Marketing Platform™. This is a subscription-based, omni-channel turnkey SRM platform that works across all top advertising, social media, and messaging networks. And it includes back-end, front-end integration, and data analytics. In time, there will be others, such as Shopify, that will offer a full suite of integrated services. SRM is headed for one-stop-shop offerings that are cheaper and easier to use. Indeed, those offerings are already coming online. The foundation for all this is in place because most companies' technologies are already driven by application programming interfaces (APIs), which employ a universal language that allows connectivity between systems. Essentially, this means that retrieving and integrating disparate data files is much easier than it was in the past. Right now, just about every major and medium-sized company can interface with the APIs of Facebook, Amazon, Google, and the new players entering the market.

We're reaching a point where any company with a merely competent technology staff (i.e., not necessarily elite analytics geniuses) can get all the same benefits as Amazon, Google, and Facebook without having to pony up the billions of dollars those companies spend. Businesses that routinely outsource search channel optimization (SCO) can do the same through monthly subscriptions to a tailor-made service that will allow them to refine their SRM efforts in ways that were impossible just a short time ago.

Moreover, businesses with these subscriptions can start to create customized self-service portals their own staff can populate and manipulate. So as employees become more familiar with the data conversion process, they can take off the training wheels and have greater freedom to drive their own interactions rather than completely outsourcing them. The analogy here might be to page-layout software, like Adobe InDesign (formerly Adobe PageMaker), which gradually allowed companies to produce their own print designs rather than simply carrying Word files to a printing company and hoping for the best. In other words, as a company's employees acquire new skills, they assume more responsibility and thus improve overall efficiency—a process that Erik Brynjolfsson and Andrew McAfee call "recombinant innovation."

Small, Medium, and Large

Businesses of all sizes recognize the importance of data analytics: 97 percent of large businesses (501 or more employees), 87 percent of medium-sized businesses (51 to 500 employees, and 57 percent of small businesses (50 or fewer employees) describe data analytics as a vital service.

Across the entire spectrum, senior US executives say that a majority of their companies' growth will depend on how well they convert raw data into actionable insights: for large businesses, the figure is 81 percent; for medium-sized and small businesses, the numbers are 65 and 50 percent respectively. Overall, that's a 49.6 percent increase from the corresponding numbers just four years ago.

When asked to specify precisely how analytics would enhance their efforts, business leaders across all size groups responded as follows:

- 79 percent said this information would enable them to better meet customer needs.
- 76 percent said it would increase sales and boost their revenues.
- 72 percent said it would expand their customer base.
- 70 percent said it would help them create better products.
- 61 percent said it would give them the capital they need to hire new employees with a wider range of skill sets.

Transformational Opportunities

Thus far in this chapter, much of what I've said about converting data to information and insights could apply to almost any business practice. I'd like to close by looking at how this conversion has special relevance to SRM efforts.

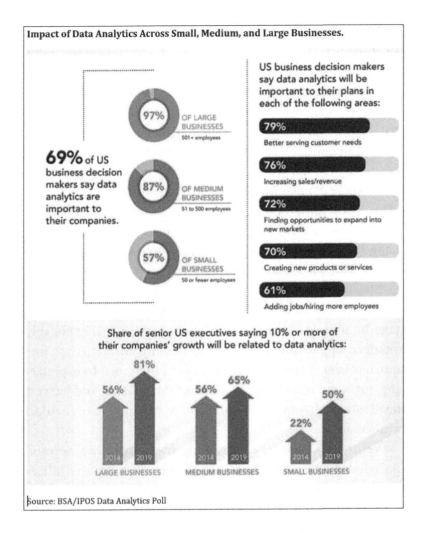

Impact of Data Analytics Across Small, Medium, and Large Businesses.

69% of US business decision makers say data analytics are important to their companies.

97% OF LARGE BUSINESSES
501+ employees

87% OF MEDIUM BUSINESSES
51 to 500 employees

57% OF SMALL BUSINESSES
50 or fewer employees

US business decision makers say data analytics will be important to their plans in each of the following areas:

79%
Better serving customer needs

76%
Increasing sales/revenue

72%
Finding opportunities to expand into new markets

70%
Creating new products or services

61%
Adding jobs/hiring more employees

Share of senior US executives saying 10% or more of their companies' growth will be related to data analytics:

81% / 56% — LARGE BUSINESSES (2014 / 2019)
65% / 56% — MEDIUM BUSINESSES (2014 / 2019)
50% / 22% — SMALL BUSINESSES (2014 / 2019)

Source: BSA/IPOS Data Analytics Poll

Earlier, when we looked at all the large insurance companies, we found almost no one had any presence on social media. This is an enormous missed opportunity, and companies who fail to exploit it should become familiar with the graph showing the decline of Motorola and Nokia in the telecommunications industry—because they are headed down the same ski slope.

The challenge is relatively minor: insurance companies want to engage consumers and sell a product; all they need to do is provide the data at their fingertips and offer instant policy quotes. Other industries do this all the time, so preservation of the status quo in the insurance industry seems suicidally and (what irony) "uninsurably" perverse. We've all seen the somewhat clever and enormously expensive TV ads by GEICO and Progressive, but how many of us have finished watching them and then gotten up to make a phone call or visit their websites? I haven't. Like most consumers, I'm not willing to work that hard anymore. Yet neither of those companies has *any* presence in SRM in messaging networks; they just use Google and Facebook as digital billboards. They could be making instant contact with a consumer who could change her car, home, and life insurance policies without cutting off her chat with a friend. But they aren't.

I can predict with 100 percent confidence that these companies will either adopt SRM practices or be shoved off the stage by upstart companies who recognize this inexplicably untapped opportunity. The established organizations are like squirrels who refuse to eat the acorns in their own tree, preferring, for some reason, to cross a busy intersection and harvest the identical nuts in a more difficult location. Lots of roadkill is inevitable.

Verishop is another company on transformational terrain. Co-founded by Imran Khan—the former chief strategy officer of Snap—the start-up has the ambitious goal of competing with Amazon. How? By *verifying* (hence *Veri*-shop) that its platform contains no counterfeit brands. Thus, it protects the retailer from brand dilution, and the consumer from paying for shoddy imitations from unauthorized sellers in Asian or Central American sweatshops. Founded in 2019, the company has already grown from absolutely nothing to tens of millions in sales each month. As of May 2020, its monthly growth rate was an astounding 33 percent.

One of Khan's key insights is that social marketing is the way of the future:

Twenty years ago, people would get their fashion tips from television or a magazine. Today, people get their news from all sorts of places, like Twitter or Instagram—and soon, it'll be some other social platform. Consumers now are influenced by all sorts of people, and they also want to be followed themselves. They want to be the leader; they want to set the fashion trend. That's a complete generational shift.[113]

Already, Verishop is using social media as a discovery platform, and it will soon be a fulfillment platform as well—so customers can browse, buy, and manage their accounts all inside social media and messaging networks. As a result, they have the potential to outcompete Amazon by being more nimble, more open-minded, more creative, and more in tune with the ideals of SRM and the emergence of The Impatience Economy.

"We let the brands tell the story and let the consumers discover the stories,"[114] Khan says. (More about storytelling in the next chapter.)

The SRM revolution is also occurring in small businesses. Consider the Stanford business school graduate who returned to his native Pakistan with the dream of serving his local community. To that end, he started an online company, through a grant from Stanford, that matches people who need domestic services with those who provide them. So when someone makes a social media request for a babysitter, he can match that person with a vetted provider, book the appointment directly in the Facebook Messenger channel, and enable instant payment. No fuss, no bother. Everyone wins.

---

[113] Emily McCormick, "E-commerce startup Verishop aims to become 'the largest online shopping mall in the Western world,'" *Yahoo Finance*, July 12, 2020

[114] Jonathan Shieber, "Imran Khan's Verishop adds Verified Shops, a way for emerging brands to set up in its digital mall," techcrunch.com, September 10, 2020

Essentially, he's recreating on a small scale an Uber or Airbnb experience for people looking for domestic work and those needing such services, but without an app! A key point here is that he initially tried to make these connections through digital ads in Google and Facebook. As soon as he shifted to SRM, the service began to achieve the lofty goals he'd set for himself.

From Amazon challengers to Pakistani micro-businesses, SRM is ushering in The Impatience Economy.

In the next chapter, we'll clarify the best ways to craft distinct SRM messages for the most popular social media channels—Facebook, Instagram, TikTok, Snapchat, and others. Too often businesses try to jigsaw their traditional marketing content into the social media puzzle. I'll help you avoid that mistake by differentiating the specific strengths and limitations of each platform. And because I'll focus on tailoring content to form, the foundational principles will apply to any new players who enter the market.

CHAPTER NINE

Storytellers Succeed: Take Your Customers on a Journey

Make Your Voice Rise

IN THE LAST CHAPTER, WE LOOKED AT HOW BUSINESSES EXtract meaningful signals from an Everest of noisy data to develop actionable insights. We've seen that empowered modern consumers resist traditional pushy marketing tactics, we've emphasized that the SRM approach demands that you establish personal two-way relationships with consumers before you attempt to sell a product, and we've shown that storytelling is the best way to establish such relationships.

The good news is that the digital marketplace gives you a microphone and an amplifier to promote your stories. The bad news? Everyone else has the same gear. If you are sitting in the center of the University of Michigan's football stadium, and everyone starts singing a different song at the top of their lungs, you won't hear 107,601 different songs. The signal of each tune will get lost in the noise of all the tunes. And since the social media "stadium" holds four billion people, the cacophony is several orders of magnitude more confusing. How in the world do you get anyone to hear you?

Don't lose heart. Your voice can rise above the others if you follow these three steps:

1. Identify a group you want to reach.
2. Find out what interests the group members.
3. Respond to those interests by developing stories optimized to specific social platforms.

The last point is crucial. Too often businesses try to jigsaw their traditional marketing content into the social media puzzle, and they fail to differentiate the specific strengths and limitations of each platform. The result is laughable when it's someone else's mistake. It's like watching a guy show up for a swim meet in soccer cleats. He won't need to worry about climbing the narrow victory platform in his wet shoes. It's also laughable when it's your mistake—except you won't be the one laughing. In what follows, I'll help you avoid that fate by clarifying the best way to tell stories on today's dominant social media platforms.

As *Break Through the Noise* author Tim Staples says, "The key is to conceptually understand the motivations and incentives that drive these platforms, to fundamentally realize what they are built to do and how they all fit together to form our social ecosystem so that you can make the system work for you."[115]

I'll start with what Tim Staples describes in his authoritative book and try to take you a step further by looking at where the platforms are heading, not just where they are today. As of this writing, for example, most social media channels are not as interactive as they soon will be. They don't let consumers click on a product to drill down for more information and thus extend their purchasing journey. Similarly, the ability to make in-channel purchases remains relatively rare. But as we saw with Chipotle, these changes are coming. And when they do, you need to be prepared

---

[115] Tim Staples and Josh Young, *Break through the Noise: The Nine Rules to Capture Global Attention* (New York: Houghton, Mifflin, and Harcourt, 2019)

because these already powerful social media platforms will then become indispensable.

YouTube

Developing a viral video could transform your business into an industry giant. And winning the lottery would allow you to move to the French Riviera and spend the rest of your life sitting on the porch of your beachfront mansion while your English butler fans you with a palm frond. Neither are realistic goals. But that doesn't mean you can't use this platform in ways that transform your business.

Why bother with YouTube? Let's start with a look at its reach:[116]

- With two billion monthly users, YouTube is the world's largest social media platform. Users upload five hundred hours of video every minute, a 40 percent increase over the past five years. Every day, users watch five hundred billion videos.
- Average users spend twelve minutes per day watching videos and open 6.5 videos every time they visit the site.
- In the US, 73 percent of adults and 81 percent of those aged fifteen to twenty-five use YouTube (the adult figure for Facebook is 69 percent).
- The platform is global: 85 percent of site usage is outside the US. 8.1 percent comes from India, and 4.6 percent, from Japan.
- Over 70 percent of YouTube views are on mobile phones, and on mobile alone, YouTube reaches more people aged eighteen to thirty-four than any TV network.

---

[116] Paige Cooper, "Twenty-Three YouTube Statistics That Matter to Marketers on 2020," blog.hootsuite.com, December 17, 2019.

So the potential audience is vast. But how do you reach it? First, forget about any traditional TV videos. No one opens YouTube to see ads. Second, keep in mind that YouTube (owned by Google), is the world's second largest search engine. Processing over three billion searches each month, YouTube has more traffic than Bing, Yahoo, AOL, and Ask.com combined.[117] This tells you that people don't come to the site to sift through random offerings, hoping to find something that catches their eye. They don't come to browse. They come with a specific purpose, and the search field lets them zero in on their target in seconds.

That's good news for you—provided you can address that purpose and offer something of value. But 98 percent of brands make the mistake of talking about themselves, like a bore at a party.[118] You can immediately separate yourself from the herd by focusing on the consumer rather than your products. Remind yourself that social media isn't TV; it wasn't designed to serve advertisers. You can't succeed in this arena unless you play by the rules of each platform.

Want a can't-miss way to develop content? Consider that how-to videos and tutorials are YouTube's third most popular content category—with twenty-four million views per month.[119] Then complete this sentence: "Consumers who use my products need help with _____." Now make a video that helps solve the problem, focusing on the issue, not your products.

One company that does this spectacularly well is AutoZone, which sells car parts to do-it-yourself (DIY) customers. The company realized that people weren't going to buy products unless they knew how to install them. So increasing the buyers' knowledge increases the company's sales. Unlike their competitors, they

---

[117] Adam Wagner, "Are You Maximizing the Use of Video in Your Content Marketing Strategy?" (Forbes, May 15, 2017)

[118] Interview with Tim Staples, "Capture Global Attention and Go Viral," LaunchStreet, August 6, 2019 (https://youtu.be/ObzeXrwXITE)

[119] L. Shannon, A. Syed, G. Anna, T. Johnstone, and K. Hanine, "YouTube: Most Popular Types/Categories," askwonder.com, December 26, 2019.

set up a YouTube channel called AutoZone DIY Garage, where consumers can learn how to install headlight bulbs, charge and test a battery, replace an alternator, and so on. In addition to a general-information series, they also provide model-specific videos. Right off the bat, they are targeting only relevant consumers, people with an interest in their products. And they aren't pushy; the only reference to AutoZone is the discreet logo on the shirt of the guy who's helping you out of a jam.

Most importantly, they are telling a story: the AutoZone mechanic has the same problem you have, and he's showing you how to fix it. Now, if you've searched YouTube for car repair advice and AutoZone carefully walks you through the process, where will you buy the parts you need? Not at Pep Boys or Advance Auto Parts. You'll order from the place with the trustworthy soul who's going to help you save money and provide backup support if you lose your way after you open the hood. Do consumers appreciate this? A number of the videos have over four hundred thousand views.

Studies show that consumers are three times more likely to watch a video that is relevant to their needs than one that stars a famous actor. Don't hire Tom Cruise to read a script about your great fan belts. Hire someone who can help your customers install them.

A final and crucial point about YouTube: if you want the algorithm to display your videos, you need to pay careful attention to your metadata (i.e., the title, keywords, tags, thumbnail photo, and description) when you upload your work. That can mean the difference between getting half a million views and getting none. Your great videos are worthless if no one sees them. I won't go into the dry specifics of how to do this, but I have a recommendation that reinforces all I've just said: when you're ready to release your content, open YouTube and search for "optimizing YouTube metadata."

Facebook

If YouTube is a goal-directed site—a digitally enhanced aggregation of an earlier generation's Yellow Pages, encyclopedias, and newspaper entertainment sections—Facebook is a kind of global pub or piazza, where consumers come to hang out, talk to their friends, catch up on issues important to them, and meet new people.[120] To succeed on either platform, businesses must appreciate this difference. On YouTube, businesses must make themselves an attractive, impossible-to-miss destination for consumers. You help *them* find *you*. On Facebook, the tables are turned: *you* must find *them*. Fortunately, no social media site offers more tools to help you make this connection.

Huge benefits accrue to those who tailor their messages to the greater informality of Facebook's platform. Worldwide, the company has 2.7 billion users, and they spend an average of fifty-eight minutes per day on the platform (thirty-eight in the US). Over 63.5 percent—about 1.5 billion—of those users log in every day to view eight billion videos and upload three hundred million photos.

---

[120] Tim Staples and Josh Young, Break through the Noise: The Nine Rules to Capture Global Attention (New York: Houghton, Mifflin, Harcourt, 2019)

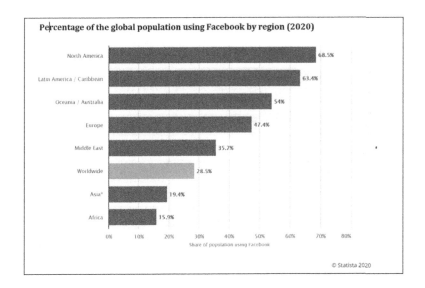

Percentage of the global population using Facebook by region (2020)

Region	Share
North America	68.5%
Latin America / Caribbean	63.4%
Oceania / Australia	54%
Europe	47.4%
Middle East	35.7%
Worldwide	28.5%
Asia*	19.4%
Africa	15.9%

Share of population using Facebook

© Statista 2020

On their own, these numbers mean very little. The BBC reaches 121 million listeners each week, but it knows almost nothing about who they are. The same is true for TV stations and newspapers. No company in history has ever *reached* more people and *gathered* as much information about them as Facebook does. For businesses, Facebook's value is its ability to aggregate, segment, and target specific types of viewers. A furniture business can instantly determine who is buying a new home. Pet supply companies can determine who has a dog, a cat, a parrot, or some combination of the three. In each case, that business can target an audience who is likely to need its products.

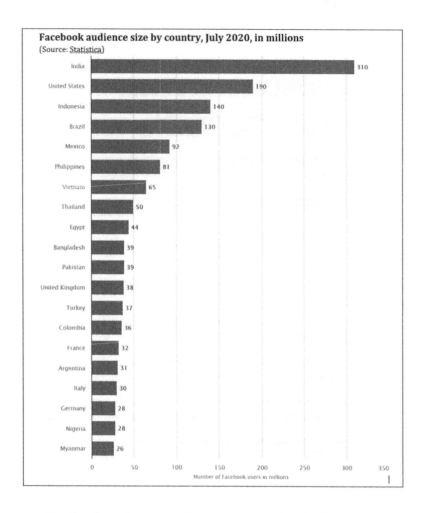

Facebook audience size by country, July 2020, in millions
(Source: Statistica)

Number of Facebook users in millions

India	310
United States	190
Indonesia	140
Brazil	130
Mexico	92
Philippines	81
Vietnam	65
Thailand	50
Egypt	44
Bangladesh	39
Pakistan	39
United Kingdom	38
Turkey	37
Colombia	36
France	32
Argentina	31
Italy	30
Germany	28
Nigeria	28
Myanmar	26

Facebook makes targeting customers simple. You just open its Ads Manager, select Custom Audience or Audience Insights, and add your product differentiators. In addition, you can set up a five-hundred-person lookalike audience—people apt to be interested in your product or service based on hidden similarities to your custom audience.

How reliable and precise is this information? Scientists at the University of Cambridge Psychometric Centre answered that question by analyzing data on more than six million platform users: "These Facebook profiles—especially people's *likes*—could be correlated across millions of others to produce uncannily accurate results. Michal Kosinski, the center's lead scientist, found that with knowledge of 150 *likes,* their model could predict someone's personality better than could their spouse. With three hundred, it understood you better than yourself. 'Computers see us in a more robust way than we see ourselves,' says Kosinski."[121]

Facebook compiles a precise portrait of each user from his or her clicks, likes, comments, movements, and networks. The irony here is that while consumers are displaying idealized portraits of themselves to their friends, Facebook's algorithms are not fooled; they see us as we really are, with all the needs, desires, and motivations we hide from ourselves and others. Scott Galloway says Facebook's "data set and targeting tools make grocery store scanners, focus groups, panels, and surveys look like a cross between smoke signals and semaphore." He adds that the company's algorithms "are the most valuable thing ever created."

Having established the platform's reach and precision, we turn to the perennial question, "How do you reach these potential customers?" Anyone who's ever walked through a street market in Cairo, Moscow, or Bangkok knows how uncomfortably pressured a consumer feels when facing someone desperate to make a sale. Every product you touch is extolled as something you can't live without or for which you can never hope to find a better price. Many tourists feel something close to fear as they try to break free from the onslaught, and they often end up retreating to their hotel's gift shop, where they gladly pay more for the same item, simply to avoid the harrowing experience. On Facebook, the circuit breaker is vastly more sensitive. Any explicit sales pitch spooks potential consumers. Nobody on social media buys out of guilt or to get the seller off her back. She simply ignores your pitch.

---

[121] Carole Cadwalldr, "Robert Mercer: The big data billionaire waging war on mainstream media," *The Guardian*, February 26, 2017

The first key to advertising on Facebook is to recognize that you have to make an instant impression. The feed-based nature of the program means that the consumer is always ready to skip ahead to the next entry. To arrest that movement, you need a riveting image and short pithy text to catch the consumer's eye. Second, you need to engage people with something they care about. Who does these things well? What models can you follow?

Consider GoPro, a company that makes action cameras and video editing software. To begin, they've carefully selected their audience, not meditation groups or card players, but skydivers, skateboarders, surfers, mountain bikers, motorcyclists, horse owners, and others who might want to film something without having to hold a camera. Next, rather than focusing on their technology, GoPro presents thrilling videos of someone racing a bike down a steep mountainside and another person diving off a cliff in Acapulco. In other words, they present precisely the kind of videos their audience wants to see—and to make. The results are breathtaking. They stop the customer's roving eye. Had they focused on the innovative lens technology developed by their no doubt brilliant engineers, GoPro would have gotten zero engagement from their adrenalized target audience. By giving their audience what it wants, they've gotten over ten million likes and forty-two thousand videos posted to their Facebook page, each made with their cameras, each a consumer-generated advertisement for GoPro. The takeaways for you: Know who you're selling to and design marketing materials that appeal to their lifestyles. Lead consumers to your products by first giving them an experience they value. Take them on a journey that doesn't begin with your product, but ends with it.

Facebook is also a great platform for storytelling. American Express does this well by presenting a collage of images and asking the consumer a question or making a simple statement. In one post, they showed an image of objects related to Christmas (e.g., red suspenders, old-fashioned boots, a compass, a list of names) and asked, "Guess whose holiday essentials these are?"

By making the answer easy—but not too easy—they encourage us to stop for a moment to solve the puzzle. They gamify the ad to capture our attention from milliseconds to seconds—that's a huge engagement increase. And in those seconds, we notice a small American Express card placed discretely—but not too discretely—in the midst of these objects. Similarly, the nonprofit organization Charity: Water, posts videos explaining how providing clean water to those in need improves the lives of millions of people around the world. They tell stories. As Dayne Topkin points out, "Business storytelling is about creating alignment between your business and your prospects and customers. This is where Charity: Water excels. They've mastered the art of storytelling to raise awareness around the global water crisis, all while inspiring people to give."[122] TOMS Shoes does something similar by showing the impact of their policy of donating pairs of shoes to needy children in Africa and Asia. The takeaway here? Use photos and video to clarify your company's values and engage consumers at an emotional and "meet the challenge" satisfaction level.

Instagram

Tim Staples calls YouTube the "public library," Facebook the "town square," and Instagram the "art gallery." So, if YouTube teaches you how to build a birdhouse, and Facebook lets you emote about how much you like the birds nesting in your creation, Instagram is where you show off your exquisite finished product—either in a compelling photo or a short video (i.e., fewer than sixty seconds). Aesthetics don't matter much when you're showing someone how to install a fuel pump, but in the art museum, they separate the winners from the also-rans. This platform demands high-quality visual storytelling. That can be a challenge, and depending on your product or service, Instagram may not be a good fit for your business.

---

[122] Dayne Topkin, "Seven Brands with Brilliant Facebook Marketing Strategies and Why They Work" (https://blog.hubspot.com/marketing/facebook-marketing-example)

But if it is, the payoffs can be enormous. Mark Zuckerberg added Instagram to his Facebook empire in 2012—at a cost of $1 billion—because he realized a basic neurological fact: we absorb images sixty thousand times faster than we do words, and they have an immediate emotional appeal that text does not.[123] As Galloway notes, on some metrics, Instagram may be the world's most powerful platform. Although it has only a third of Facebook's users, it generates fifteen times the level of engagement. Consider the following 2020 Instagram statistics:[124]

- One billion people use Instagram every month, and 630 million log in every day.
- Users spend an average of twenty-eight minutes per day on the platform.
- Instagram's potential advertising reach is 849.3 million users, a 6 percent increase from 2019.
- More than five hundred million Instagram users open its Explore tab every month to discover new content, and 62 percent say they have become interested in a brand after clicking the Stories tab.
- Most important of all, Instagram Shopping now allows users to *buy products without leaving the social media channel.* More than 130 million consumers purchase products this way every month.

---

[123] Ritu Pant, "Visual Marketing: A Picture Is Worth 60,000 words," *Business 2 Business Community,* January 16, 2016

[124] Christina Newberry, "37 Instagram Stats That Matter to Marketers in 2020," October 22, 2019 (https://blog.hootsuite.com/instagram-statistics/)

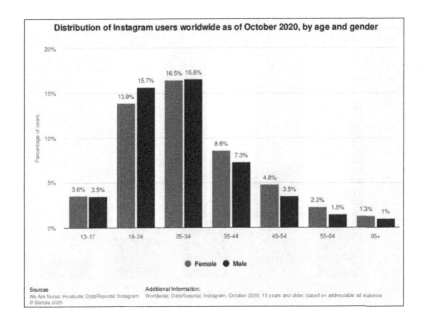

Distribution of Instagram users worldwide as of October 2020, by age and gender

Female   Male

Sources
We Are Social; Hootsuite; DataReportal; Instagram
© Statista 2020

Additional Information:
Worldwide; DataReportal; Instagram; October 2020; 13 years and older; based on addressable ad audience

The new Shoppable Stories feature places Instagram in the vanguard of the digital retail revolution. Not only do businesses engage consumers in a narrative, they also enable them to buy the products they see with nothing more than a swipe. This is a giant leap forward in Social Retail Marketing. Businesses should prepare themselves to take advantage of this new shopping model, which is certain to proliferate across all platforms in the next few years. Adidas, Louis Vuitton, and the clothing company Aritzia all provide excellent storytelling models you can adapt to your own business.

Snapchat

Snapchat is in the challenging position of being compared to Instagram. Owned by Snap Inc., the messaging app lets users exchange photos and videos (i.e., snapshots) that disappear shortly after they are viewed. Because of its array of filters to customize and distort images in playful, often irreverent ways, the company has always been most popular with young users.

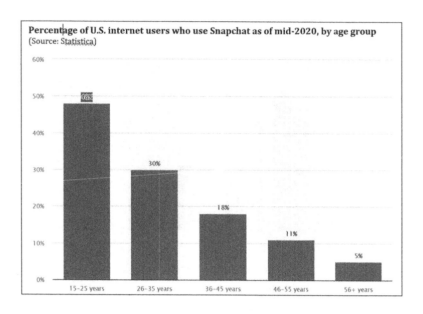

Percentage of U.S. internet users who use Snapchat as of mid-2020, by age group (Source: Statistica)

In 2017, Galloway offered a terse assessment of how the Snapchat-versus-Instagram rivalry would end: "Facebook . . . positioned itself to crush the young company. I believe the first thing Mark Zuckerberg thinks when he opens his eyes in the morning, and the last as he closes them at night is, 'We're going to wipe Snap Inc. off the face of the planet.' And he will."

Zuckerberg has failed to do so, and my money is on Evan Spiegel and his team. My view is that Snapchat will not just survive, but also thrive in ways the market doesn't understand yet. I believe Snapchat's 2018 partnership with Amazon will be a fundamental catalyst in the changing calculus. The partnership was ahead of its time and offers an excellent example of SRM in action. What's innovative here is that Snapchat users simply hold up their mobile device, scan an image or a barcode of something they want to buy, and snap a photo. If it's available an Amazon, a digital card will appear, and the consumer can click through to Amazon and make a purchase.

"Consumers are increasingly being served up ads on social media, but shopping directly from popular apps has been slow to catch on, hindered by technology that takes too many steps," says Laura Heller a *Forbes* contributing writer. "But this new tool . . . could help to change that. Shopping via social media is now significantly more likely to drive purchases, particularly with younger shoppers, who are more likely to be heavy users of both Instagram and Snapchat. For Snap, there's a clear goal of boosting revenue, but for Amazon, the payoff is likely more complex, which is true of most [of] Amazon's initiatives."[125]

As of 2019, Snapchat had 186 million daily users, compared to 400 million for Instagram.[126] In 2020, Snapchat had a 26.3 percent mobile audience reach in the US, ranking behind Facebook, Instagram, and Facebook Messenger—and its share of the key teenage demographic was slipping.[127] However, in The Impatience Economy, the Snapchat-Amazon partnership is an excellent example of how Social Retail Marketing is changing the marketplace. And I predict we'll see Snapchat's performance metrics begin to increase decisively.

What companies are using the channel effectively to create stories that reach this audience? Both Taco Bell and Sour Patch Kids have done model work in using Snapchat Stories, which allows businesses to combine multiple snaps and thus extend conversations beyond the platform's original ten-second limit. Taco Bell has used this format to help consumers get Valentine's Day dates, and Sour Patch Kids added 120,000 new Snapchat followers by posting engaging videos starring an amusing, life-sized "Blue Kid."[128]

---

[125] Laura Heller, "Amazon and Snapchat Form a Powerful Partnership," *Forbes*, September 26, 2018

[126] Russ Shumaker, "Snapchat vs. Instagram: The Main Differences You Need to Know and Why," marketingsfgate.com, January 3, 2019

[127] J. Clement, "Snapchat usage penetration in the United States 2020, by age group," *Statistica*, September 23, 2020

[128] Sujan Patel, "7 Brands That Are Killing It on Snapchat," *Entrepreneur*, February 6, 2017 (https://www.entrepreneur.com/article/286147)

TikTok

As the *New York Times* reports, "TikTok will change the way your social media works—even if you're avoiding it."[129] While TikTok's future remains uncertain as of late 2020, *Forbes* notes that the video app is unlike any other social media platform—and it has no clear rivals in the current marketplace.[130] Like YouTube, TikTok offers a repository of videos—except they are all short, and consumers don't arrive, as at a library, with a clear sense of what they want. Rather than steering a search engine, TikTok users tend to follow wherever the algorithm leads. Content discovery is the platform's central attractor. It also attracts a lot of consumers:[131]

- In the four years since its release, the app has been downloaded more than 1.9 billion times.
- In the US, more than three hundred million monthly users watch thirty-seven billion videos.
- The average US user spends forty-six minutes per day on the app.
- More than half of all US users are under twenty-five. Those who are eighteen to twenty-four account for 42 percent of use, and those who are thirteen to seventeen account for 18 percent.
- US consumers aged thirteen to twenty-six are just as likely to use TikTok as Facebook or Twitter.
- Perhaps most important for businesses, TikTok engagement rates are significantly higher than those for Instagram or Twitter.

---

[129] John Herman, "How TikTok Is Rewriting the World," *The New York Times*, March 10, 2019

[130] Andrea Bossi, "There Are 3 Clear TikTok Competitors, But None Are Close To Dethroning It," *Forbes*, August 24, 2020

[131] Katie Sehl, "Everything Brands Need to Know about TikTok in 2020," blog. hootsuite.com, March 2, 2020

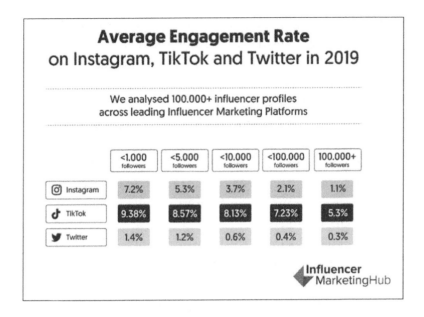

Average Engagement Rate
on Instagram, TikTok and Twitter in 2019

We analysed 100.000+ influencer profiles
across leading Influencer Marketing Platforms

	<1.000 followers	<5.000 followers	<10.000 followers	<100.000 followers	100.000+ followers
Instagram	7.2%	5.3%	3.7%	2.1%	1.1%
TikTok	9.38%	8.57%	8.13%	7.23%	5.3%
Twitter	1.4%	1.2%	0.6%	0.4%	0.3%

Influencer
MarketingHub

How fast is TikTok taking off? Influencer Katie Sehl explains:

> The Washington Post hired a TikTok app expert. Buzzfeed is recruiting teens to cover elections on TikTok. According to *The Verge,* Justin Bieber is desperate for his single "Yummy" to go viral on TikTok. A who's-who of celebrities, including everyone from Snoop Dogg to Reese Witherspoon, have opened accounts. And ads finally made their way onto the platform, *along with a shoppable component.*

That last sentence holds the most significance for businesses. Beyond the various video filters, music options, and other bells and whistles, what changes our lives is the consumer's ability to shop inside the channel—as we saw with Instagram. The shopping feature is called Hashtag Challenge Plus, which prompts consumers to post videos of themselves using a product. A separate tab lets viewers buy any product they see. In essence, the TikTok user shows off her creativity by making a video with a product, prompting all her viewers to buy, and it also provides them with the means of doing so. What's not to like?

Kroger was the first business to participate in the campaign, which prompted college students to make videos of their dorm rooms. While watching, viewers could click-and-buy the various Kroger products that appeared in the video (e.g., snacks, a toaster, a popcorn maker, and so on). The student videos received 477 million views, the vast majority from a similar cohort with the same purchasing interests.

In late 2020, TikTok partnered with Shopify—an e-commerce platform that allows over one million businesses of all sizes to set up an online store and sell, ship, and manage their products. Shopify's goal is to reach TikTok's younger audience. By installing the TikTok app, Shopify sellers will be able to use the "TikTok for Business Ads Manager," which will enable them to target audiences by gender, age, and purchasing behavior and to evaluate the impact of various marketing campaigns over time. "The TikTok channel means Shopify merchants—even those without a strong TikTok following of their own yet—can connect with these new audiences using content that feels authentic and genuine to the TikTok experience," says Shopify vice president of product Satish Kanwar.

"We are delighted to partner with Shopify and provide a channel for their merchants to reach new audiences and drive sales," says Blake Chandlee, TikTok's vice president of global solutions.

> As social commerce proliferates, retailers are recognizing that TikTok's creative and highly engaged community sets it apart from other platforms. We're constantly exploring new and innovative ways to connect brands with our users, and Shopify is the perfect partner to help us grow and expand our commerce capabilities globally.

Sarah Perez, a reporter for *TechCrunch*, adds that "TikTok and Shopify's partnership won't be limited to the new TikTok channel app. That's just the first step."

> The deal will soon expand to other shopping features too. TikTok says it plans to start testing new in-app features that will make it easier for users to discover Shopify merchants and their products by expanding their reach through video and on their account profiles. These features will also let users browse merchants' products and *shop directly through the TikTok app.*[132]

The Second Consumer Revolution is here! And SRM is the present and future of retail and marketing.

In the next chapter, we'll look at three barriers to the rapid progression of The Impatience Economy and Social Retail Marketing. More specifically, we'll explore the need for businesses to embrace cross-industry opportunities; for businesses and governments to safeguard consumer trust, privacy, and confidence; and for government regulators to find the sweet-spot between protecting consumers and encroaching on their freedoms.

---

[132] Sara Perez, "TikTok partners with Shopify on Social Commerce," https://techcrunch.com/2020/10/27/tiktok-invests-in-social-commerce-via-new-shopify-partnership/, October 27, 2020

CHAPTER TEN

The Goldilocks Zone: Regulating The Impatience Economy™

Earn Consumer Confindence

IN PREVIOUS CHAPTERS, WE'VE LOOKED AT THE ENORMOUS power that will accrue to buyers during the Second Consumer Revolution. In this chapter, we'll examine the most serious obstacles to the rapid progress of that revolution, as well as the steps necessary to avoid those setbacks and delays that will work to the detriment of both consumers and businesses.

All these delays are avoidable, but not without collective action. At present, most businesses focus too narrowly on their individual enterprises and ignore their shared responsibility for creating a consumer-friendly marketplace that spans the entire digital landscape. This insular approach may yield a few short-term benefits, but the ultimate consequence of an every-person-for-themselves attitude will be to cut corners in ways that lower consumer trust and retard progress. Although we have not yet reached a tipping point on this front, worrisome signs are already evident, and without immediate action, they will only get worse. No single business can solve this problem. A small percentage of malefactors can tarnish the reputations of all the players—just as a single company pumping pollutants into the air can put everyone at risk. Moreover, unless we regulate ourselves, we can expect heavy-handed government regulations that may end up punishing consumers in the name of protecting them.

A 2019 survey shows a disturbingly wide disconnect between business and consumer perceptions about the security of the digital marketplace: while 70 percent of businesses think the consumer is "very confident" to "extremely confident" in their ability to protect private information, only 28 percent of consumers actually feel this way. In other words, businesses are overrating consumer confidence (and their own performance) by 60 percent. Perhaps even more alarming, consumers are eight times more likely to say they have no confidence in businesses' safeguards than those businesses realize. Unless businesses adjust to this reality, they risk being in the unenviable position of a confused pilot, betrayed by his senses, flying nose down through the clouds while imagining he is headed for the blue sky above them.

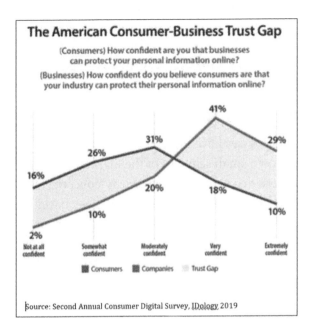

The American Consumer-Business Trust Gap

(Consumers) How confident are you that businesses can protect your personal information online?

(Businesses) How confident do you believe consumers are that your industry can protect their personal information online?

Source: Second Annual Consumer Digital Survey, IDology 2019

The "trust gap" must be closed. Allowing matters to drift along in this uneasy status quo presents one set of dangers. Inviting governments to unilaterally intervene with ill-informed, draconian regulations that reduce consumer freedom presents another. In what follows, I'll chart a third way that avoids both those risks—increasing consumers' freedoms without jeopardizing their peace of mind. More specifically, I'll look at three fundamental challenges:

1. Big tech and other businesses must abandon their current inward-looking strategies for an outward-looking approach that embraces cross-industry opportunities to create a consumer-friendly marketplace.

2. Business leaders must recognize they are underestimating consumer concerns, and enact policies to restore trust.

3. CEOs must work to avoid unilateral government regulations that curtail consumers' individual freedoms, and promote a multilateral strategy that expands them.

No Company Is an Island

Too often businesses have focused narrowly on short-term interests in their own small segment of the market. They've neglected the consumer's privacy and data security concerns. The absence of regulations has enabled them to do so. They haven't taken the time or expended the effort to look beyond their own verticals and ask large, difficult cross-industry questions about data collection, privacy, credential management, consumer rights, and digital identity.

This is shortsighted. In an earlier age, unregulated businesses pumped pollutants into the air and water as though a day of reckoning would never come. Upton Sinclair's muckraking *The Jungle* exposed the way Chicago meat-packers routinely disregarded public safety in pursuit of quick profits. By behaving as if they were indifferent to large-scale social costs, by failing to take preemptive action that could have protected the public and still allowed them to profitably serve consumers, these industries squandered consumer trust and forced governments into an adversarial stance, filling the void left by business neglect with well-intentioned but suboptimal policies.

This failure is a textbook instance of what economists call the "tragedy of the commons."[133] In the classic example, members of a rural society cut and gather firewood from common lands to which they all have equal access. It's in no individual's rational short-term interest to invest in these lands since he will bear the full weight of the cost, but reap only a small fraction of the benefit. But by pursuing his own self-interest, each person behaves

---

[133] Garrett Hardin, "The Tragedy of the Commons," *Science*, December 13, 1968

contrary to the common good. Over time, the land on which all depend becomes degraded by their collective action. Everyone suffers.

As Dennis D. Hirsch points out in a *Duke Law Journal* essay, "Privacy, Public Goods, and the Tragedy of the Trust Commons," consumer trust (like common lands) is a perishable resource that can be degraded when individual businesses act to maximize their own short-term rewards, lose sight of the common good, and ignore the negative impact of their collective actions. The misuse of personal information will lead to what Hirsch calls a tragedy of the "trust commons":

> The information economy is premised on the sharing of personal information; it is "mediated by information relationships" to a far greater extent than prior economies. Participating in the information economy accordingly requires us to trust others with our personal information. This particular kind of trust—"digital trust"—consists of our faith that the providers of digital goods and services will use our personal information to benefit—not hurt—us.[134]

CPAs and physicians recognize that no matter how principled most practitioners may be, the behavior of a few outliers can erode public trust in their profession as a whole. As a result, those professions established licensing boards and codified best practices. In the digital economy, businesses need to be similarly farsighted, looking beyond the isolated silos of their own activities and asking what they can do collectively to protect and serve consumers. They should recall that both the Great Depression (1929–1933) and the Great Recession (2007–2009) resulted in

---

[134] Dennis, D. Hirsch, "Privacy, Public Goods, and the Tragedy of the Trust Commons," *Duke Law Journal*, February 2016, Volume 65

part from a loss of public trust. Should the same happen to the digital trust that drives the information economy, the financial consequences will be catastrophic—and a great opportunity will be squandered.

How great? Consumers have indicated that if their privacy concerns were allayed, they would spend an additional $6 billion online.[135] The graph below clarifies the dramatic difference between the rising fortunes that result from collective actions that produce a resilient consumer "trust commons" and the collapse that results from a myopic self-centered (or industry-specific) approach.

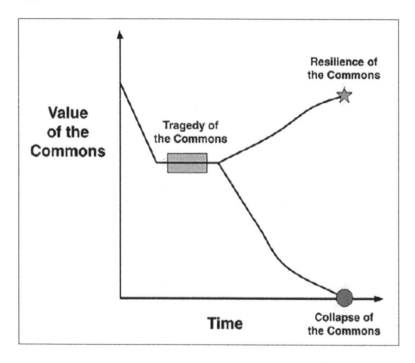

The key takeaway here is that businesses need to do what

[135] Jonathan W. Palmer, Joseph B. Bailey, and Samer Faraj, "The Role of Intermediaries in the Development of Trust on the WWW: The Use and Prominence of Third-Parties and Privacy Statements," March 3. 2000 (http://jcmc.indiana.edu/vol5/issue3/palmer.html)

they've resisted doing: open up a dialog among a wide range of industries, consumer protection advocates, and government officials to see how they can improve the security, peace of mind, and freedom of their customers. Failing to do so will all but ensure unilateral government intervention, which, as we will see, is unlikely to produce outcomes that serve any of the players in the digital ecosystem.

The State of Consumer Trust

A Pew Research Center study found that consumers' willingness to share personal information depends on whether the benefits outweigh the risks.[136] Participants worried about the safety and security of their information and expressed anger and confusion about the ways in which companies use it. Business leaders should be especially concerned by the finding that these concerns are growing more pronounced.

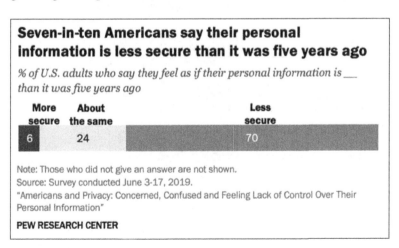

Seven-in-ten Americans say their personal information is less secure than it was five years ago

% of U.S. adults who say they feel as if their personal information is ___ than it was five years ago

More secure	About the same	Less secure
6	24	70

Note: Those who did not give an answer are not shown.
Source: Survey conducted June 3-17, 2019.
"Americans and Privacy: Concerned, Confused and Feeling Lack of Control Over Their Personal Information"

PEW RESEARCH CENTER

Indeed, 70 percent of those surveyed, feel that their personal

---

[136] Lee Rainie and Maeve Duggan, "Privacy and Information Sharing," *Pew Research Center* (2016)

information is *less secure* than it was five years ago—and of the remaining 30 percent, only one-fifth (i.e., 6 percent of the total) felt it was more secure, with 24 percent saying it was "about the same." More troubling still, results show consumers' mistrust isn't confined to the limitations of the technology, but extends to the companies who use it: 79 percent of Americans doubt that businesses would admit to misusing their data, 69 percent suspect their data is being used in ways they don't approve of, and 65 percent have little confidence that companies would notify them if their data were compromised.

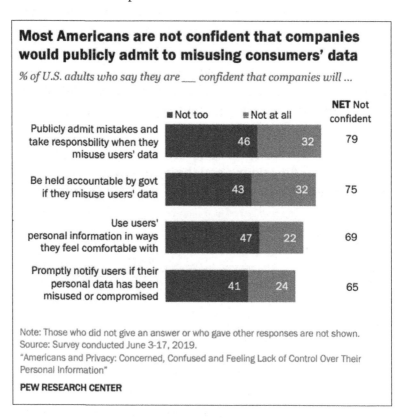

Most Americans are not confident that companies would publicly admit to misusing consumers' data

% of U.S. adults who say they are ___ confident that companies will ...

	■ Not too	▨ Not at all	**NET** Not confident
Publicly admit mistakes and take responsbility when they misuse users' data	46	32	79
Be held accountable by govt if they misuse users' data	43	32	75
Use users' personal information in ways they feel comfortable with	47	22	69
Promptly notify users if their personal data has been misused or compromised	41	24	65

Note: Those who did not give an answer or who gave other responses are not shown.
Source: Survey conducted June 3-17, 2019.
"Americans and Privacy: Concerned, Confused and Feeling Lack of Control Over Their Personal Information"

PEW RESEARCH CENTER

Consumers also express anxiety about who can access their online activities: 85 percent of US social media users feel they have little or no control over who can view their posts, and 87 percent express similar concerns about private texts. For website visits and search terms, the corresponding figures are 90 and 91 percent.

Let's look at one of these, access to search terms, to see why consumers might be concerned and what new ethical dilemmas such access might raise. Recent research by Microsoft shows that it can match the prediagnosis search history of pancreatic cancer patients to searches by people in the early stages of the disease and make increasingly reliable predictions about their ultimate fate. To the extent that this information might enable a patient to seek early treatment for a disease in which late treatment rarely succeeds, this big data insight looks like an unalloyed blessing. At the moment, however, nothing prevents the company from selling such information to insurance companies, who could then raise the patient's rates—before she even knows she has the disease. HIPAA rules protect the privacy of medical information, but no such rules apply to search histories.[137]

---

[137] Alina Selyukh, "Can Web Search Predict Cancer? Promise and Worry of Big Data & Health," npr.org, June 10, 2016

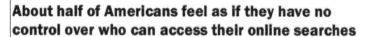

About half of Americans feel as if they have no control over who can access their online searches

% who say they feel___ control over who can access the following types of their information

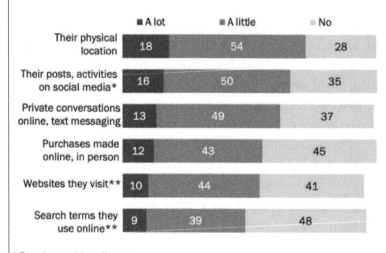

	A lot	A little	No
Their physical location	18	54	28
Their posts, activities on social media*	16	50	35
Private conversations online, text messaging	13	49	37
Purchases made online, in person	12	43	45
Websites they visit**	10	44	41
Search terms they use online**	9	39	48

* Based on social media users.
** Based on internet users.
Note: Respondents were randomly assigned questions about how much control they feel they have over who can access different types of their information. Those who did not give an answer are not shown.
Source: Survey of U.S. adults conducted June 3-17, 2019.
"Americans and Privacy: Concerned, Confused and Feeling Lack of Control Over Their Personal Information"

PEW RESEARCH CENTER

Clearly, trust on the digital commons is under threat, and unless we act, advances in technology will exacerbate those threats in ways that are impossible to foresee. In the next section, we'll look at how to reduce those threats in ways that serve consumer confidence and freedom.

Enlightened Regulation

Anyone who's ever watched a congressional panel discuss technology issues could be forgiven for thinking that enlightened internet and data security policies have about the same chance of emerging from these representatives—working on their own—as would a responsible set of aviation standards from Samuel Adams, John Jay, and the other members of the First Continental Congress. "Elected officials and their staffs are not tech savvy enough to understand the scope of the problems," Lawrence Norden of the Brennan Center tells *Scientific American* in an article on "congressional ignorance" about cybersecurity issues.[138] *TechCrunch* journalist Devin Coldewey is more caustic: after watching a House of Representatives meeting, he complained of members "airing musty arguments and grandstanding generically as if they had just been informed about the existence of the internet."[139]

My own views are somewhat more hopeful. I've seen governments step up and do an effective job of regulating the telecommunications industry. Did they have a deep understanding of the technology? No. But they understood what was good for the consumer, what was good for protecting privacy—and they balanced those concerns with what was good for the economy and what would promote innovation. For example, the government saw that roaming rates were a huge scam. For no reason whatsoever, companies would charge more if you used your phone outside your area or country. All the mobile phone companies knew the government would eventually regulate and eliminate those rates because there was no sustainable logic behind them; they were just a moneymaking mechanism. But guess what? Businesses kept charging until the very last moment—until the government finally said, "*No más*. This has to stop. You guys are gouging the

---

[138] Jackson Barnett, "Congressional Ignorance and Leaves US Vulnerable to Cyberthreats," *Scientific American*, October 21, 2019
[139] Devin Coldewey, "Congress Flaunts Its Ignorance in House Hearing on Net Neutrality," techcrunch.com, February 7, 2019

consumer." But in the process of delaying, companies made huge amounts of money at the expense of consumers. And the mistrust that grows out of that kind of experience accounts for part of the reason why 51 percent of people feel tech companies need more regulation than they currently receive, and only 9 percent feel that they need less. And this isn't some issue that divides sharply along stereotypical political lines (i.e., with Democrats favoring regulation and Republicans opposing it). Only 12 percent of Republicans and 7 percent of Democrats think tech companies should be less regulated.

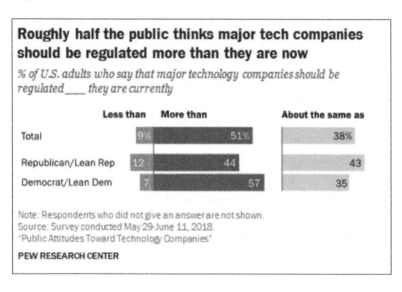

Roughly half the public thinks major tech companies should be regulated more than they are now

% of U.S. adults who say that major technology companies should be regulated____ they are currently

	Less than	More than	About the same as
Total	9%	51%	38%
Republican/Lean Rep	12	44	43
Democrat/Lean Dem	7	57	35

Note: Respondents who did not give an answer are not shown.
Source: Survey conducted May 29-June 11, 2018.
"Public Attitudes Toward Technology Companies"

PEW RESEARCH CENTER

Governments have the responsibility to protect the public and create a level playing field. We shouldn't be naive. We don't live in an age where people think, *What's good for General Motors, Facebook, YouTube, and Twitter is what's good for America.*

Having said that, however, I want to stipulate three qualifications. First, governments need to make data security issues a priority. They haven't yet shown much willingness to do that. Rather than targeting fundamental issues, they've taken an ad hoc approach, ignoring the big picture and instead dealing with whatever happens to be of interest to this or that investigator or subcommittee—or to any individual with enough influence to drive a grassroots movement on some tangential subject. For the Second Consumer Revolution to flourish, governments need to drop this reactive approach and adopt proactive strategies. They need to stop pulling out the duct tape every time the ceiling springs a leak, and start thinking about the general condition of the roof.

Second, governments lack the expertise to do this on their own. Regulating the technology industry effectively demands a cooperative effort from all the players in the market—just as any attempt to regulate new medicines requires biologists and prospective patients, and any attempt to explore nuclear power options requires physicists and homeowners adjacent to reactor sites. If I were in charge, I would set up a summit meeting tomorrow and bring together consumer advocate groups, government policymakers, leaders of various social media platforms, and those CEOs who have adopted SRM strategies. And we'd make progress—because at the end of the day, everyone wins if we develop checks and balances that benefit consumers, protect their rights, promote their confidence, and increase their freedoms. To act otherwise is akin to poisoning the well on which the whole ecosystem depends—and inviting a regulatory backlash that hurts everyone.

A 2019 survey by CISCO shows that consumers favor this multipronged approach to protecting privacy, one in which governments play a *key* role, but not an *exclusive* one. Though the largest group of respondents (46 percent) said governments have primary responsibility for protecting privacy, the combined totals for consumers (24 percent) and companies (21 percent) exactly match the figure for governments (i.e., 46 percent).

Third, and most important, governments should focus on large-scale framework issues rather than operational details. In this, I'm following the distinction between "formal law" and "substantive rules" established by Nobel Prize–winning economist Friedrich Hayek:

> The distinction . . . between formal law or justice and substantive rules is very important and at the same time most difficult to draw precisely in practice. Yet the general principle involved is simple enough. The difference between the two kinds of rules is the same as that between laying down a Rule of the Road, as in the Highway Code, and ordering people where to go; or, better still, between providing signposts and commanding people which road to take.[140]

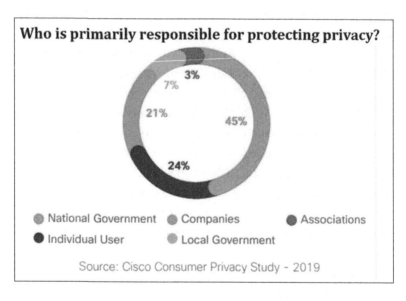

Who is primarily responsible for protecting privacy?

3%
7%
21%
45%
24%

- National Government
- Companies
- Associations
- Individual User
- Local Government

Source: Cisco Consumer Privacy Study - 2019

Hayek unpacks this metaphor by describing how, in the name of consumer protection, government intervention often encroaches on our basic freedoms. The title of his book—*The*

---

[140] F.A. Hayek. *The Road to Serfdom*, (Chicago: University of Chicago Press, 1944)

Road to Serfdom—indicates his view of where such encroachments eventually lead:

> The state should confine itself to establishing rules applying to general types of situations and should allow the individuals freedom in everything which depends on the circumstances of time and place, because only the individuals concerned in each instance can fully know these circumstances and adapt their actions to them. If the individuals are to be able to use their knowledge effectively in making plans, they must be able to predict actions of the state which may affect these plans.... Hence the familiar fact that the more the state "plans," the more difficult planning becomes for the individual.

How do we apply Hayek's "formal law" to government action with respect to data security and privacy? What "signposts" should government post on our digital turnpikes? First and foremost, we need laws to protect a consumer's *digital identity*. These are long overdue. Protecting a consumer's social security number, credit card information, bank account details, and passwords—these are all vital to a person's well-being. Without such protections, any digital transaction is perilous. Who wants to share their profile if the security of this information is at risk? *I* certainly don't. No sane person does. Governments need to step in and establish regulations here the same way they need to post ONE WAY (à) street signs to prevent head-on collisions. Without a shared set of expectations, many people will stop pulling out of their digital driveways. We need to reach the point where people don't worry about their data being breached any more than they worry about their lives being at risk every time they step onto an airplane, or that the canned food they bought at the grocery store is going to give them botulism.

Thomas Edison said that successful inventors need "a good imagination and a pile of junk." Until recently, businesses have treated consumers' personal information—what Harvard professor Dr. John Brownstein calls their "digital exhaust"—as a pile of junk. But oil was junk before we learned to harness its power, silicon chips would have been junk to Genghis Khan, and Edison's junk turned to gold once he assembled it into a telephone and a light bulb. Modern digital technologies have alchemized once-useless consumer data in a similar fashion. Consumers may not have realized that early on, but the cat is now out of the bag. We all see that businesses monetize our digital profiles. Apple, Google, Facebook, Samsung, and others—they are all drilling for oil on our land, we get nothing in return, and legislators are turning a blind eye. Why shouldn't consumers get upset?

Now, if you're really appalled, can you deny access to your information, your digital identity, to companies? People who don't trust banks can stuff their money in their mattresses. Fair enough. It's a free country. But I'm certain the vast majority of consumers will be willing to part with their information if they can do so safely, and, eventually, if they are compensated for it: "You want my oil? OK, but first, don't let it leak into my groundwater, and second, you need to give me something in return." You grant Facebook, for example, permission to use your profile, but you demand something like a credit to spend on music or whatever else you want to buy digitally. That changes the paradigm; you're telling companies that access to your data is a *privilege*, not a *right*.

This is an example of what I call the "big rules" and what Hayek calls the "formal law." Only governments can establish these regulations—and to do so effectively, they need to collaborate with consumers and businesses so they increase safety and fairness without stifling innovation and freedom. That's a difficult balance, but these goals shouldn't be mutually exclusive.

And under wise stewardship, they won't be. Once we strike that equilibrium, The Impatience Economy will proceed as reliably as a law of physics.

Now, just as enlightened governments should assert themselves in big-picture situations, they will also absent themselves from small matters. Punishing businesses from co-opting a consumer's digital identity for private gain is one thing. Restricting access to information a consumer chooses to share in exchange for specific benefits is something quite different. The first is a clear-cut protection from harm; the second is an equally clear-cut example of paternalism, an encroachment on basic freedoms—a wolf in sheep's clothing. The government justifiably sets speed limits to protect drivers from themselves and others. It doesn't ban left turns, set highway speeds at twenty miles per hour, or require you to take a specific path to the supermarket because that route is 0.0001 percent safer than the one you prefer. For the vast majority of digital interactions, enlightened governments will trust the free market to work out the best compromises. Such governance is a necessary condition for unleashing the profound benefits of patience Economy and Social Retail Marketing.

Again, Hayek provides a clarifying insight:

> While every law restricts individual freedom to some extent by altering the means which people may use in the pursuit of their aims, under the Rule of Law, the government is prevented from stultifying individual efforts by ad hoc action. Within the known rules of the game, the individual is free to pursue his personal ends and desires, certain that the powers of government will not be used deliberately to frustrate his efforts.

In warning against the dangers of government overregulation, Hayek, Friedman, and other free-market advocates are simply endorsing the ideal Thomas Jefferson expressed in his first inaugural address: "A wise and frugal government . . . shall restrain men from injuring one another, shall leave them otherwise free to regulate their own pursuits of industry and improvement . . ." Free to regulate their own pursuits of industry and improvement, as long as it doesn't cause harm to one another. This preamble is as powerful today as it was in 1801, 220 years ago.

So just as Goldilocks, when she entered the bears house, had to try the three porridges, the three chairs, and the beds, to find the ones that were *just right*, finding this regulatory Goldilocks zone—neither too laissez-faire nor too paternal—will determine whether we rapidly unlock the full benefits of the Second Consumer Revolution or stagnate for years in a self-lacerating and unproductive status quo.

Dalibor Vavruska has recently taken a big step in this direction by introducing a new national digital governance framework, the Digital Nation Model (D-NA), which "endorses separation of network infrastructure from services, alongside separation of heavily regulated data/services from lightly regulated ones, creating three independent layers: 1) infrastructure; 2) licensed data, cloud, and digital services; and 3) open market data, cloud, and infrastructure services."[141] Vavruska emphasizes the centrality of this challenge: "Our future depends on our conscious choices of which technologies we develop, deploy, constrain, and potentially suppress; how we control them; whom and what we connect; how we choose to balance power with accountability; which society values we protect; and which ones we knowingly forego. Possible scenarios include the following:

- States will proactively oversee the adoption of crucial new technologies; they will support personal, economic, and

---

[141] Dalibor Vavruska, *Empowering Nations in a Digital Age: A New Data and Digital Governance Framework for the 21st Century* (Digiteccs, 2020)

innovative freedoms while assuring that any entities empowered by data and AI are accountable through transparent governance frameworks; they will decisively intervene in carefully selected areas to protect humans, their ways of governance, their societal values, and environment.

- The uncontrolled global spread of technologies and data-driven AI systems will lead to divergence between power and accountability, major disruptive changes to the economic and political order, profoundly impacting national sovereignty and other core society values.
- A combination of the two, possibly leading to conflict."

If you are reading this book and have stayed with it this far, by definition, you are a player in the digital ecosystem. It is up to you, consumers, businesses, governments, to take action to ensure we end up with the proper balance and mechanism to calibrate it as necessary over time.

In the next chapter, we'll look at how consumers will discover and buy inside social media and messaging channels, where—in The Impatience Economy—people make their decisions to buy or move on more quickly than an eyeblink. We'll also see how successful marketers create, track, refine, and iterate—and how platforms like Google, Facebook, Salesforce, Hootsuite, HubSpot, FastFoward.ai, and others give businesses the tools they need to sell to digital and social consumers. We'll look deeper under the hood of Social Retail Marketing.

CHAPTER ELEVEN

Faster! SRM™ and the New Science of Buying

Pattern Recognition

I N William Gibson's futuristic science fiction novel *Pattern Recognition,* Cayce Pollard has a supernatural, 100 percent reliable, and extremely profitable gift for understanding "the semiotics of the marketplace": she can tell in an instant whether a logo or design will resonate with consumers or leave them cold and unresponsive.[142] She has no way of explaining how she makes these determinations. Nor can she instruct companies about how to modify their failed efforts to make them successful. Like a Roman emperor determining the fate of a gladiator, she gives either a thumbs-up or a thumbs-down: yes or no, life or death. This skill earns her vast sums of money because she prevents companies from making ruinous marketing investments.

Pollard's fanciful gift belongs under the second term of the compound science fiction genre. If you're still hoping a telepathic marketing employee can boost your sales, you've not been reading

---

[142] William Gibson, *Pattern Recognition* (New York: Penguin Random House, 2003)

carefully. Why look for a clairvoyant to improve your business, when you can use A/B testing to eliminate guesswork with data-driven solutions? Why pay for what Gibson calls a "sensitive" like Pollard? The Create-Track-Refine-Iterate™ model can help you systematically zero in on optimal product designs and marketing strategies? Why not leave "pattern recognition" to the computer scientists who coined the phrase, allowing them to extract action-able business insights from the mountains of consumer data no human mind could ever hope to parse?

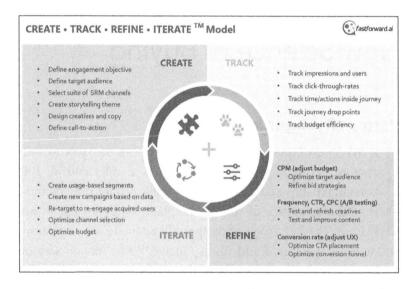

If you dismiss Gibson's invention of a mystical seer (and you should), the process by which she works contains a kernel of truth for businesses trying to prosper in patience Economy: though none of us can extrapolate our specific product reactions to all con-sumers, we all make satisfying, split-second personal purchasing decisions, and—like Pollard—we're often unable to explain pre-cisely why we did so—though we sometimes articulate a rationale after the fact. Understanding the various complex micro-points that precede a sale has spawned a number of new and overlap-ping fields of study: perceptual psychophysics, neuromarketing, consumer neuroscience, neurobiological decision-making, and persuasion science.

In this chapter, we'll look at the implications of these findings for SRM, for unless we understand the psychological substrates of buying behavior, our marketing efforts will be wasteful and imprecise. We'll also look at the revolutionary insight of Nobel Prize–winning psychologist Daniel Kahneman: most of our purchasing decisions are driven by rapid but reliable and informed *intuitions* rather than by a long and laborious chain of time- and energy-consuming analysis. In the process, we'll see that the SRM model of establishing emotional connections with consumers offers the best (and only) way of converting Kahneman's insight into business success. Throughout the COVID-19 pandemic we've been exhorted to "trust the science." CEOs hoping to thrive in The Impatience Economy need to take that same advice as they form their marketing plans.

Blink

Research on the "psychophysics of perceptual judgments" and the "computational and neurobiological basis of decision-making" has shown that "consumers can make decisions in as little as a third of a second . . . and a significant fraction of decisions seems to be made at these speeds." That's only slightly longer than an eyeblink. The authors conclude, "these results suggest that consumers make accurate everyday choices, akin to those made in a grocery store, at significantly faster speeds than previously reported."[143] These findings support my earlier contention that the seemingly simple acts of leaving a social media feed, opening a separate app (e.g., Amazon's), and then navigating to find and buy

---

[143] Milica Milosavljevic, Christof Koch, and Antonio Rangel, "Consumers can make decisions in as little as a third of a second," *Judgment and Decision Making*, Volume 6, Number 6, August 2011

a product create an increasingly sale-breaking friction point for consumers in the Age of Impatience.

Of course, the dark converse of the researchers' point is also true: sellers who don't make their products instantly available for purchase inside social media platforms will lose sales. The same speed-driven consumer who makes a millisecond decision to *buy* a product will also be making a millisecond decision to *reject* that same product if the time constraint is too great. The second hand of a clock is no longer sufficient to calculate your margins of success or failure. Today, you need a digital stopwatch. The graph below indicates that the minimum reaction time our brains need to make accurate product comparisons is 313 milliseconds (ms). "Saccades" (on the Y axis) are quick, simultaneous movements of both eyes.

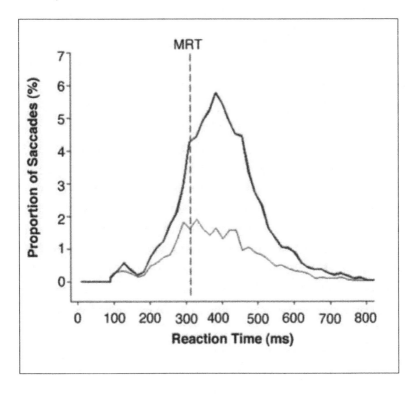

As Malcolm Gladwell has pointed out in his bestselling *Blink*,[144] the rapidity of a decision doesn't mean that it is inaccurate or uninformed. Indeed, the theme of his book is that "decisions made very quickly can be every bit as good as decisions made cautiously and deliberately." He describes, for example, how a team of lawyers and scientists had spent months authenticating an $10 million Greek statue later purchased by the J. Paul Getty Museum. Just prior to its unveiling, several experienced art critics glanced at the statue and had an immediate, intuitive sense that it was a fraud. Something looked amiss—though they couldn't say precisely what. They were right. Based on a millisecond-long glimpse, they were better consumers than Getty's entire team. "Have you paid for this?" one of the critics asked the museum's board members. When they looked stunned, he added, "If you have, try to get your money back. If you haven't, don't."

The insightful critics "didn't weigh every conceivable strand of evidence," Gladwell notes.

> They considered only what could be gathered in a glance. Their thinking was what the cognitive psychologist Gerd Gigerenzer likes to call "fast and frugal." They simply took a look at that statue, and some part of their brain did a series of instant calculations, and before any kind of conscious thought took place, they felt something.

And that feeling pointed them to the truth.

The key takeaway for SRM purposes is this: experts in a field—and all consumers are intuitive experts about their own desires—can make instantaneous decisions by relying on what social psychologist Daniel Wegner calls the "adaptive unconscious," a relatively new field of psychology with special relevance

---

[144] Malcolm Gladwell, *Blink: The Power of Thinking without Thinking* (New York: Little, Brown, and Company, 2007)

to marketers. Forget what you know about Freud's nonscientific view of the dark id-driven unconscious. Wegner's is a pragmatic, quantifiable entity. He maintains that a consumer's brain is like a computer that can draw on a lifetime's worth of stored (i.e., adaptive) preferences, automatically analyze a new object, and make a millisecond-long assessment about whether she is interested or not. The buyer doesn't need to sit for thirty minutes and ask herself, "What do I think of this pair of shoes?" The adaptive unconscious—which is running every second of our lives—takes a time- and energy-saving shortcut that spares us these deliberations. It knows what we like and produces an immediate and reliable emotional reaction. The art critics who assessed the fraud didn't generate a checklist of logical explanations but had an immediate visceral response that logic could later redundantly confirm. One critic reacted to the statue with an "intuitive repulsion," a feeling that preceded any thought.

Our conscious minds eventually take us to the same destination, but emotion gets there first. Gladwell describes a fascinating experiment that demonstrates this point, one that no marketer should ignore. Students asked to evaluate a teacher based on three two-second video clips produced the exact same assessments as did students who sat through an entire semester with that teacher. Like the students, consumers are equipped with the same high-speed assessment skills. Marketers who behave as if purchasing decisions begin with long and tediously rational deliberations should plan to lose a lot of business to competitors whose ads spark the quick interest of the adaptive unconscious. And because SRM builds *emotional* connections with consumers, it is the ideal strategy for applying Wegner's insight.

Readers might stop for a moment here, and ask themselves why they decided to purchase this book. Did you sit down and list the pros and cons of this decision? Of course you didn't. Time is money, and you'd never get anything done if you behaved like that. Would a blunt message from my publisher, saying, "You need Augie Fabela's book! Buy it now!" have overcome your hesitation? Not a chance. Instead (be honest!) the vast majority of you glanced at the title, sensed that it accurately captured the shifts you've noticed in the marketplace, scanned the table of contents or a blurb on the back cover, felt an emotional connection with the topic, and (if you've read this far) immediately made a wise decision about how to prepare yourself to profit in a complex and evolving Impatience Economy. Keep in mind your own prepurchase chain of actions as you adjust next year's marketing plan. Let your own behavior serve as a proxy for the behavior of your consumers. They aren't aliens you need to decode. They're just like you. To modify a line from Sir Philip Sydney, you can look in your heart, and . . . sell.

System 1 Thinking: Emotions and Sales

As Harvard Business School professor Gerald Zaltman points out in *How Consumers Think: Essential Insights into the Mind of the Market*,[145] 95 percent of purchasing decisions are driven by split-second *emotional* choices that draw on the wisdom acquired during the buyer's lifetime of experiences. When a musician plays an improvisational piece, she isn't making consciously structured, effortful, moment-by-moment decisions, nor is she ineptly winging it, as a novice would be forced to do. Instead, she knows that the skills she's built through a lifetime of diligent practice will produce a spontaneous emotional reaction consistent with her musical ideals. Consumers behave with this same virtuosity. Like Garry Kasparov playing speed chess or a shortstop reacting to the crack of the bat, they behave both wisely and quickly. Marketers who approach consumers with condescending tutorials on why they need to buy a product, who treat buyers as shopping novices rather than as adepts, will evoke a trio of negative reactions: irri-

---

[145] Gerald Zaltman, *How Consumers Think: Essential Insights into the Mind of the Market* (Cambridge, Massachusetts: Harvard Business School Press (2003)

tation, boredom, and avoidance. It's hard to justify a marketing budget that pays off in those counterfeit currencies.

Both Gladwell and Zaltman are popularizers building on the intellectual foundation established by Daniel Kahneman, especially his insight about System 1 and System 2 thinking, which earned him a Noble Prize.[146] To simplify it a bit, System 1 describes the rapid, intuitive analyses we've discussed above, and System 2 describes the slower, more painstaking process we employ when facing questions our brains have not evolved to perform (e.g., What's 17 x 319?). Kahneman's key insight is that System 1 thinking is not only crucial to our survival, but that it governs the vast majority of our decisions—including our purchasing behavior—far more than most of us credit. He notes that System 2 is lazy, almost always defers to System 1, and often simply provides after-the-fact rationalizations for the rapid and generally wise choices we've already made.

As *The Economist* reports, Kahneman's paradigm has had revolutionary implications for businesses: "Kahnemanite advertising prizes emotion" and "appeals to System 1's propensity to respond to subtle cues." How subtle? A version of a pie advertisement with "the fork placed on the right triggered a 20 percent higher 'purchase intent' than one with the fork on the left (because most people eat with their right hands)."[147] The editors note that this kind nuance "demands not just new ways of making adverts, but new methods for judging if they will work." They add that "researchers must 'laser in on measuring *emotion* as almost the single metric' that predicts success." Paraphrasing Kahneman, they point out that "even information-packed adverts that seem to be appealing to reason are really playing on emotions."

---

[146] Daniel Kahneman, *Thinking, Fast and Slow* (New York: Farrar, Straus, and Giroux, 2013)

[147] The editors, "Advertising: Nothing More Than Feelings, The Economist, December 7, 2013.

That this should be so conforms to the views of renowned neuroscientist Antonio Damasio, who argues that "feelings have not been given the credit they deserve" as the fundamental drivers of consumers' "motives, monitors, and negotiators."[148] We don't need to grasp the synaptic-level biophysical reactions that support Damasio's claim to benefit from his insights. For marketing purposes, we can cut to the key point in his *Descartes' Error: Emotion, Reason, and the Human Brain*[149]—that the rationalist French philosopher's famous dictum, "*Cogito, ergo sum*" ("I think, therefore I am"), might more accurately be stated, "I feel, therefore I am."

Damasio's point is not that feelings are antirational. Quite the contrary. When we instantly pull our hand from a hot stove, when our feelings of loneliness prompt us to call a friend, or when we feel the urge to buy a new product because it would increase our pleasure or reduce our pain, we are acting in our own self-interest.

What's often ignored, however, is the orderly chain of reactions that precede a sale: feelings precede emotions, and emotions precede thoughts. Once the process starts, we enter a feedback loop in which emotion-driven thoughts further escalate our emotions. The problem, Damasio says, is that in retracing this pattern, we often see thoughts as the starting line. They aren't. When you carefully review the roster of micro-points that precede a sale, the igniting spark is always an emotion. Businesses that fail to appreciate this are like mystery writers who tear out the first two chapters of a carefully plotted novel, and then wonder why readers don't respond to their work. SRM avoids this mistake because it always begins at the beginning—with the emotional connection— that precedes (and motivates) the final call to action.

---

[148] Antonio Damasio, *The Strange Order of Things: Life, Feeling, and the Making of Cultures* (New York: Vintage Books, 2019)

[149] Antonio Damasio, *Descartes' Error: Emotion, Reason, and the Human Brian* (New York: Avon Books, 1994)

Drop the Status Quo: Cadbury's Gorilla

In 2007, the Cadbury chocolate company—known for its conservative approach to marketing—contacted the Fallon London agency about developing a video ad that could help the company recover from a disastrous 2006, in which one of its products was contaminated with salmonella, resulting in a damaged image, a 5 percent decline in sales, and a fine of over $1 million.[150] Fallon's creative director, Juan Cabral, recommended an emotional appeal to System 1 thinking: eating chocolate makes people feel good, and the ad should do the same. In essence, Cabral sought to turn the company from "chocolate makers to producers of happiness." He advised the company not to "*tell us* about joy, but *show us* joy." Cadbury agreed to that general strategy.

They were less agreeable about the way Cabral chose to implement it. The entire ninety-second ad consists of a gorilla sitting at a drum set and eventually playing wildly along to Phil Collins's 1981 hit "In the Air Tonight." Only in the final moments does the company's logo appear. When Cadbury executives watched the piece, they thought Cabral had lost his mind. "Let's get this right," one of them said. "You want us to run an ad that's three times longer than a normal, has no Cadbury's chocolate in it, and contains no message?"[151] Another executive abandoned the sarcastic interrogative for a blunter response: "You are *NEVER* showing this ad!"

Cabral stood by his guns, however, insisting that, as a first step, "a brand needs to go to the heart and not to the brain" and asserting that the unconventional ad would "rekindle the love" of their customers. Eventually, he persuaded Phil Rumbol,

---

[150] "Case Study on Cadbury's Gorilla Advertisement," https://www.google.com/amp/s/mbasean.wordpress.com/2014/11/15/case-study-on-cadburys-gorilla-advertisement/amp/

[151] Quotes throughout this section are from Jo Caird, "I was basically told, 'You are never showing this'—How we made Cadbury's Gorilla ad, The Guardian, January 7, 2016.

the director of Cadbury's marketing team, who in turn swayed the reluctant executives to take a chance. With a great deal of tension in the air (the entire boardroom of monetarily stifled voices waiting to scream, "I told you so"), the company aired the ad.

Cabral's instincts were correct—and they've gradually reshaped advertising ever since. In 2015, *Marketing* magazine named the ad the nation's all-time favorite.[152] It went viral on YouTube and won the marketing industry's biggest prize, a Film Grand Prix Lion at the Cannes Lions International Advertising Festival. But it wasn't just an aesthetic triumph. "Everyone celebrated it creatively," says Rumbol. "What gets talked about less is how effective it was from a business point of view. Having persuaded the people at Cadbury to do the ad, the return on investment was three times the normal level."

Cabral's approach is perfectly aligned with the strategy I'm advocating for SRM. It offers something of value to consumers (in this case, entertainment) and doesn't simply try to *explain* how good its products are or (worse) force chocolate bars down viewers' hesitant throats. In Kahneman's terms, it puts emotional connection before sales, it respects consumers, and it trusts their System 1 reactions. Despite some initial reluctance, Cadbury showed the kind of innovative courage all businesses will need to muster in The Impatience Economy. The company bucked what *The Economist* called the erroneous, old-school "conventional wisdom," which "doubted that a jolt of joy from a drumming primate, however rhythmically gifted, would spur the sales of chocolate bars." And that courage paid off: Cadbury's profits jumped by 10 percent after they unloosed their inner gorilla.

We all need to fight the status quo!

---

[152]   https://www.campaignlive.co.uk/article/cadburys-gorilla-nations-favourite-ad-industry-opts-guinness-surfer/1364711?src_site=marketingmagazine

Images Are Key

Research shows that social media posts must instantly grab consumers' attention or they will move on to something else. Visuals communicate more far more quickly than text. Consider the following graphic from NeoMam Studios:[153]

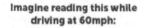

In Social Retail Marketing, businesses need to learn from the DMV, and treat consumers as motorists rushing along an interstate highway. Your social media posts may be as elegantly written as one of Shakespeare's sonnets, but your potential customers have neither the time nor the inclination to admire your handiwork. Aim for road signs, not rhymed couplets. That I've chosen to *show* the image above rather than *describe* it demonstrates my point.

The data supports what the image depicts:[154]

- Our brains can understand an image in one millisecond. Reading a two-hundred-word description of that image takes sixty thousand times longer (i.e., a minute).
- Visual memories are stored in the same part of our brains where we process emotions. Thus, they more effectively engage the System 1 circuitry that Kahneman sees as the starting point for purchasing decisions. This point is easy

[153] Danny Ashton, "Ten Reasons Why Visual Content Marketing Works," NeoMam. com, February 19, 2015. The photograph of the woman below appears in this essay.
[154] Melanie Tamble, "Seven Tips for Using Visual Marketing," Social Media Today, February 20, 2019

to prove. Which do you find more moving, the photo on the left or the text on the right? If Doctors Without Borders were trying to increase donations to treat infant mortality, which should they use?

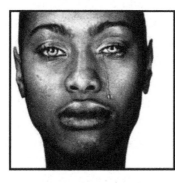

A woman stares directly into the cam while a single tear rolls down her che

- We recall visual information six times faster than information we hear or read. That's because 50 percent of our brains are devoted to image processing, and 70 percent of our sensory receptors are in our eyes.
- Social media posts with images attract 12 percent more traffic and promote 200 percent more shares than those without images.
- Content with relevant images receives 94 percent more views than content with generic images.
- On Twitter, tweets with images attract 18 percent more clicks and 150 percent more retweets than those without.
- Facebook posts with images generate 3.2 times more engagement than those without.
- LinkedIn posts with images attract a 98 percent higher comment rate.
- In 2021, more than 75 percent of all data traffic will consist of videos.[155]

---

[155] Cisco Annual Internet Report (2018-2023) White Paper, March 20, 2020 (https://www.cisco.com/c/en/us/solutions/collateral/executive-perspectives/annual-internet-report/white-paper-c11-741490.html)

In his scholarly analysis of "Starbucks' Marketing Communications Strategy on Twitter,"[156] Viriya Taecharungroj notes that the main purpose of the company's emotion-evoking content is to create positive feelings: happiness, excitement, awe, serenity, peacefulness, calmness, and delight. Photos and video are the most effective way to achieve this end. But his final point is crucial for an effective SRM campaign: "These images are typically beautiful, digitally adjusted (filtered), and/or modified to create interesting spectacles for audiences." Starbucks does more than simply post an image of a smiling coffee drinker. They take hundreds of photos using dozens of models, adjust minute details of color and shading in Photoshop, and A/B test those results to design an optimal campaign.

The payoff? "The visual modality leads to higher average numbers of both retweets (1,267 versus 767) and favorites (3,432 versus 1,525) than the textual modality," says Taecharungroj. "The effect is the most prominent in action-inducing content, in which the visual modality generates much higher average numbers of retweets (3,964 versus 946) and favorites (5,615 versus 1,403). He concludes, that"

> Although action-inducing content is the most effective in generating high numbers of retweets and favorites, a strong interaction effect indicates that visual content significantly improves effectiveness whereas textual content does not significantly improve the effectiveness of the tweet.

In other words, emotion-generating visuals motivate consumers to act in far greater numbers than does text.

---

[156] Viriya Taecharungroj, "Starbucks' Marketing Communications Strategy on Twitter," *Journal of Marketing Communications*, 2016

Profits and the Emotionally Connected Consumer

Two studies from the *Harvard Business Review* emphasize the following counterintuitive point:

> Our research across hundreds of brands in dozens of categories shows that the most effective way to maximize customer value is to move *beyond mere customer satisfaction* and connect with customers at an *emotional level*—tapping into fundamental motivations and fulfilling their deep, often unspoken emotional needs. That means appealing to any of dozens of "emotional motivators," such as a desire to feel a sense of belonging, to succeed in life, or to feel secure.[157]

The key point here is that many businesses may be able to deliver a satisfying product, but far fewer make a systematic effort to establish the fully satisfying emotional bond crucial to maximizing profits. Because social media's raison d'être is emotional expression and connection, the SRM approach I've advocated throughout this book enables you to take that next step.

And taking it pays huge dividends. In "The New Science of Customer Emotions," Magids, Zorfas, and Leemon show that businesses content with "highly satisfied customers" leave a lot of money on the table: "Although brands may be liked or trusted, most fail to align themselves with the emotions that drive their customers' most profitable behaviors." They add that "a company doesn't have to be born with the emotional DNA of Disney or

---

[157] See Alan Zorfas and Daniel Leemon, "An Emotional Connection Matters More than Customer Satisfaction," the *Harvard Business Review*, August 29, 2016; and Scott Magdis, Alan Zorfas, and Daniel Leemon, "The New Science of Customer Emotions," the Harvard Business Review, November, 2015

Apple" to achieve this alignment. "Even a cleaning product or a canned food can forge powerful connections."[158]

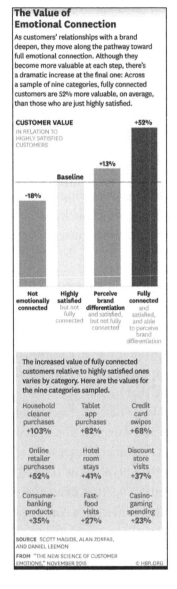

The Value of Emotional Connection

As customers' relationships with a brand deepen, they move along the pathway toward full emotional connection. Although they become more valuable at each step, there's a dramatic increase at the final one: Across a sample of nine categories, fully connected customers are 52% more valuable, on average, than those who are just highly satisfied.

CUSTOMER VALUE
IN RELATION TO
HIGHLY SATISFIED
CUSTOMERS

			+52%
		+13%	
	Baseline		
-18%			
Not emotionally connected	Highly satisfied but not fully connected	Perceive brand differentiation and satisfied, but not fully connected	Fully connected and satisfied, and able to perceive brand differentiation

The increased value of fully connected customers relative to highly satisfied ones varies by category. Here are the values for the nine categories sampled.

Household cleaner purchases +103%	Tablet app purchases +82%	Credit card swipes +68%
Online retailer purchases +52%	Hotel room stays +41%	Discount store visits +37%
Consumer-banking products +35%	Fast-food visits +27%	Casino-gaming spending +23%

SOURCE SCOTT MAGIDS, ALAN ZORFAS, AND DANIEL LEEMON

FROM "THE NEW SCIENCE OF CUSTOMER EMOTIONS," NOVEMBER 2015   © HBR.ORG

What are the benefits of doing so? On average a "fully connected" online retail consumer is 52 percent more valuable than a "highly satisfied" one—and for some industries, the figure is as high as 103 percent. Not only do such consumers buy more of your products and services, they exhibit less price sensitivity, pay more attention to your communications, follow your advice, and recommend you more—everything you hope their experience with you will cause them to do. Moreover, the researchers found that "customers become more valuable at each step of a predictable 'emotional connection pathway' as they transition from (1) being unconnected to (2) being highly satisfied to (3) perceiving brand differentiation to (4) being fully connected." Indeed, customers become 18 percent more valuable simply by moving from step 1 to step 2 and an additional 13 percent from step 2 to 3. Across the entire four-step emotional spectrum, customer value increases by an astonishing 70 percent.

One problem businesses face, however, is the following:

---

[158] Scott Magids, Alan Zorfas, and Daniel Leemon, "The New Science of Customer Emotions," the *Harvard Business Review*, November, 2015

Identifying and measuring emotional motivators is complicated, because *customers themselves may not even be aware of them.* These sentiments are typically different from what customers *say* are the reasons they make brand choices and from the terms they use to describe their emotional responses to particular brands. [That's why] companies should pursue emotional connections as a science—and a strategy.

High-Impact Motivators

Hundreds of "emotional motivators" drive consumer behavior. Below are 10 that significantly affect customer value across all categories studied.

I am inspired by a desire to:	Brands can leverage this motivator by helping customers:
Stand out from the crowd	Project a unique social identity; be seen as special
Have confidence in the future	Perceive the future as better than the past; have a positive mental picture of what's to come
Enjoy a sense of well-being	Feel that life measures up to expectations and that balance has been achieved; seek a stress-free state without conflicts or threats
Feel a sense of freedom	Act independently, without obligations or restrictions
Feel a sense of thrill	Experience visceral, overwhelming pleasure and excitement; participate in exciting, fun events
Feel a sense of belonging	Have an affiliation with people they relate to or aspire to be like; feel part of a group
Protect the environment	Sustain the belief that the environment is sacred; take action to improve their surroundings
Be the person I want to be	Fulfill a desire for ongoing self-improvement; live up to their ideal self-image
Feel secure	Believe that what they have today will be there tomorrow; pursue goals and dreams without worry
Succeed in life	Feel that they lead meaningful lives; find worth that goes beyond financial or socioeconomic measures

SOURCE SCOTT MAGIDS, ALAN ZORFAS, AND DANIEL LEEMON

Simply asking consumers what drives their emotional connections is a fool's errand, like asking someone to account for precisely why he loves his wife and children. The emotions are real, but don't expect to unveil them in a questionnaire. Can you offer a precise reason for why you've selected your close friends? Can you account for the differences between recent acquaintances you feel emotionally connected to and those you simply like? Your failure doesn't invalidate the feelings or the closeness, but it does prevent you from typing out a kind of friendship job description you can hand out to people you meet. That kind of connection reveals itself *experientially* and can't be translated into words by even the most nuanced writer.

That's why I've been touting the importance of data analytics, which present deeper insights into how consumers behave rather than relying on how they say they behave. That's why we all need to keep abreast of advances in the new science of neuromarketing, which can identify the biological substrates of purchasing decisions—those that exist outside the bounds of everyday awareness. That's why SRM connections are essential to the future of your business, because they access truths you can't access any other way.

Hurry Up! SRM Response Times Are Crucial

We opened this chapter by looking at consumers' millisecond-long purchase decisions. We'll close by looking at what impatient consumers expect from businesses communicating within an SRM channel. But as you might have guessed, if you want to establish the kind of bond we've been discussing, faster is better.

As of 2020, 44 percent of US consumers expect a social media response to a question or a complaint in an hour or less, and 75 percent expect a response within a day. Worldwide, the latter figure is 83 percent. These expectations make it clear that consumers expect business to uphold the *social* proprieties of a social media relationship.

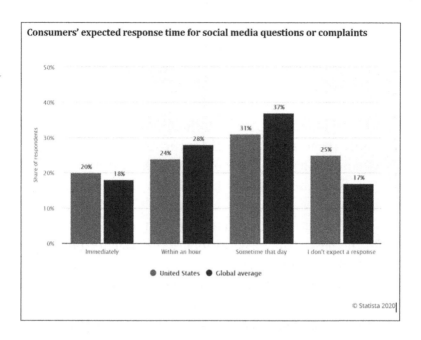

Consumers' expected response time for social media questions or complaints

- United States
- Global average

© Statista 2020

To benefit from SRM connections, sellers need to honor their part in the conversation just as they would if the consumer were sitting across the desk from them. Texas State University's Raymond Fisk points out the following:

> Social media provides new tools for marketers, but ensuring value requires following the old rules of human conversation. Conversations require taking turns and listening respectfully while the other person is speaking. Old broadcast media were one-way communication tools that made it easy for marketers to shout at customers but hard to listen to them. Social media are two-way communication tools that make it easy for organizations to talk to customers, for customers to talk to each other, and to listen to them. Customers will value those organizations that listen and respond

to their complaints, praise, and requests. They will tell their friends if they like you, which ensures even more value. Smart organizations will join the conversation.[159]

They certainly will. A study by Juniper Research showed that consumer spending inside social media chatbots—which have been dramatically upgraded to offer more lifelike conversations—will increase from $2.8 billion in 2019 to $142 billion in 2024, an increase of 4,971 percent.[160] For businesses that adopt the SRM strategies I've described, the future can't get here fast enough!

In the next chapter, I'll introduce the Digital Consumers' Bill of Rights, designed to be foundational protections for digital consumers without infringing upon their freedoms, and giving consumers control over their privacy; digital identity; and what, when, where, and how they consume everything and anything they want. Getting this social contract right and finding the proper balance of government and self-regulation, what I call the *just-right* "Goldilocks Zone," is fundamental to the prosperity of The Impatience Economy.

---

[159] Quoted in Kent Huffman's *Eight Mandates for Social Media Marketing Success* (Austin, TX: C-Suite Press, 2012)

[160] Robert Williams, "Facebook researchers detail progress in contextual chatbots for shopping" marketing.dive.com, June 5, 2020

CHAPTER TWELVE

The Digital Consumers' Bill of Rights™

Foundational Protections

WHEN ASKED TO LIST AMERICA'S FOUNDING FATHERS, most of us call to mind six names: Jefferson, Hamilton, Madison, Franklin, Washington, and Adams. But students of history know that George Mason deserves to be included in that list. The Virginian, whom Jefferson called "the wisest man of his generation," not only penned some of the most memorable phrases in the Declaration of Independence, but also, his retort, "I would sooner chop off my right hand than put it to [i.e., sign] the Constitution as it now stands," led directly to the creation of the Bill of Rights,[161] which limited the newly established government from restricting the freedoms of US citizens and which remains perhaps the most important of our foundational documents.

Historian Robert Rutland notes the following:

---

[161] Lisa Gold, *Forgotten Founders: George Mason*, baumanrarebooks.com, October 24, 2013 (https://www.baumanrarebooks.com/blog/forgotten-founders-george-mason-part-2-1787/)

Federalist supporters of the Constitution could never overcome the protest created by Mason's phrase: "There is no Declaration of Rights." Months later, Hamilton was still trying "to kill that snake" in Federalist No. 84. . . .

But the idea was too powerful. . . .

Not long after Mason's pamphlet reached Jefferson's desk in Paris, the American minister was writing to friends at home in outspoken terms. Jefferson told Madison he liked the Constitution but was alarmed by "the omission of a bill of rights," which . . . the people are entitled to against every government on earth . . . and what no government should refuse or rest on inference.[162]

Having explored the qualities that constitute The Impatience Economy (i.e., its "constitution"), I'd now like to follow Mason—though without offering to chop off my hand—by proposing a Digital Consumers' Bill of Rights that will allow The Impatience Economy and Social Retail Marketing to flourish. Just as a new country needs to establish foundational protections for its citizens to thrive, the new economy, accelerated by the COVID-19 pandemic, creates an urgent demand to codify a set of principles to guide businesses and enable consumers to prosper.

And make no mistake; we are living through a revolutionary moment, the Second Consumer Revolution. As Scott Galloway notes in his *Post Corona: From Crisis to Opportunity*, in March 2020, we were living in a *before* era. By the end of the month, we had entered an *after* stage: "A virus one four-hundredth the width

---

[162] Robert Allen Rutland, *The Birth of the Bill of Rights: 1776 to 1791* (New York: Collier Books, 1966)

of a human hair grabbed a sphere weighing thirteen billion trillion tons and set it spinning ten times faster."[163] The change has been as dramatic as if we'd been struck by a giant meteorite; shifts that would have taken decades were now occurring in weeks. E-commerce's share of the retail market had been growing by one percent per year from 2000 to the start of 2020. By January of 2020, about 16 percent of retail was conducted through digital channels. Eight weeks after the pandemic hit, that number had increased by 69 percent. That's ten years of e-commerce growth in fifty-six days.

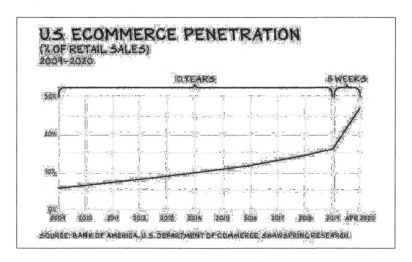

It's as though we had suddenly been thrust into 2030, equipped with flying cars but with no air traffic control system to guide their movement.

My goal in this chapter is to provide that kind of guidance so that buyers and sellers can maximize the benefits of The Impatience Economy without imploding due to misguided self-interest or, as I explained earlier, the digital commons. I'll focus on the following preamble and five inalienable rights:

---

[163] Scott Galloway, *Post Corona: From Crisis to Opportunity* (New York: Penguin Random House, 2020)

The consumers of the world have an inalienable right to digital expression, privacy, and ownership of our individual digital identity. We also have the right to choose what, when, where, and how we consume in our pursuit of convenience, lifestyle, peace of mind, and freedom.

1. The first right is to freely express our views online without being censored by the prevailing sentiment exercised by the ruling bodies of government or business.
2. The second right is to own our digital identity, actions, and behaviors. Our consumer data cannot be used without consent and fair-value exchange.
3. The third right is to defend our privacy through encryption and intellectual property (IP) rights over our own data and consumption behavior.
4. The fourth right is the freedom to choose, allowing us to control what, when, where, and how we consume anything and everything.
5. The fifth right is to not have our aforementioned rights infringed upon by paternalistic government regulations or restrictive business policies.

The through line connecting these rights is my vision of a trustworthy digital commons in which all participants understand and honor the same set of rules. Unless consumers feel safe enough to express their ideas freely—without self-censorship or fear of reprisal—businesses will be unable to anticipate their needs and help them discover new products and services. Similarly, if consumers are wary about how businesses use their data, they may choose to withhold it completely—depriving themselves of myriad benefits, and depriving producers of enormous profits. Moreover, in a landscape of mistrust, governments will likely step in to "fix" problems they are ill-equipped to understand, creating a situation in which everyone suffers. My Digital Consumers' Bill of Rights seeks to establish a set of guardrails that will prevent these and other problems, allow the free market to bestow benefits on buyers and sellers, unleash the full potential of our revolutionary moment, and discover the new and fruitful opportunities that can emerge from the pandemic crisis—provided we look beyond the tragedy to the opportunities it has created.

As George Mason said in response to an earlier challenge, if we behave with enlightened foresight, "a few years' experience will convince us that those things which at the time they happened we regarded as our greatest misfortunes have proved our greatest blessings."[164]

Does this sound like 1801 or 2021 to you?

The First Right

The first right is to freely express our views online without being censored by the prevailing sentiment exercised by the ruling bodies of government or business.

How important is the freedom to express ourselves online and to be free from censorship by either tyrannical majorities or the shifting sentiments of governments or businesses? Consider the following statement from legal scholar and longtime American Civil Liberties Union (ACLU) president Nadine Strossen:

> Social media [has] become the dominant platform for the exchange of information and ideas. In fact, the US Supreme Court recognized in a unanimous opinion in 2017 that the social media platforms are the most important platforms for the exchange of information and ideas and communication, not only among all of us as individuals

---

[164] Kate Mason Rowland, *The Life of George Mason, 1725-1792*, Volume 2 (Charleston, SC: Nabu Press, 2012)

with our friends and family members, but also between us and government officials and politicians. So, it's really important not only for our individual freedom of speech to be meaningful, but also for our rights as citizens in a participatory democracy to have equal access to social media platforms. That is why so many people, so many government officials, so many human rights agencies and activists are thinking very hard and working to implement ways to protect equal and fair access to social media platforms for all of us, even if our ideas are unpopular or controversial.[165]

The Congressional Research Service echoes this point in its 2019 report "Free Speech and the Regulation of Social Media Content":

One of the core purposes of the First Amendment's Free Speech Clause is to foster "an uninhibited marketplace of ideas," testing the "truth" of various ideas "in the competition of the market." Social media sites provide one avenue for the transmission of those ideas. The Supreme Court has recognized that the internet in general, and social media sites in particular, are "important places" for people to "speak and listen," observing that "social media users employ these websites to engage in a wide array of protected First Amendment activity."[166]

[165] Nadine Strossen, "Does the First Amendment Apply to Social Media Companies" (https://www.talksonlaw.com/briefs/does-the-first-amendment-require-social-media-platforms-to-grant-access-to-all-users)
[166] Valerie C. Brannon, "Free Speech and the Regulation of Social Media Content," The Congressional Research Service, March 27, 2019.

For SRM to reach its full potential as a public good, government needs to establish some basic regulations, not for the sake of Orwell's Big Brother, not to restrict the free market, but for the sake of the consumer—to protect safety and equal access, to safeguard individual users from potential abuses by companies or various bad actors. We have these kinds of regulations in other industries—telecommunications, oil, electricity, transportation, and financial services—but we lack the equivalent for big data and social media. The industry is too new. As a result, companies can make their own rules about what we can see, forward, and discover; they can restrict free access across a channel based on their taste, political bias, or capricious sense of right and wrong. SRM cannot reach its full potential under such shifting and unpredictable conditions.

To be clear, I'm not advocating large-scale government intrusion. Rather, I side with Milton Friedman's view that "government's role is to serve as an *umpire* to prevent individuals from coercing one another," not to serve as either a participant or "as a parent charged with the duty of coercing some to aid others."[167] Just as driving needs clear rules of the road to protect citizens and prevent accidents, so SRM needs to codify and enforce a set a of business regulations so the new economy can flower. And only government can serve in this role—just as in, say, the oil industry, where the government sets a basic framework that protects the interests of the consumer and society from potentially unfair or dangerous actions by Exxon Mobile, Chevron, and other energy giants.

The Economist makes this clear in its October 24, 2020, cover story, "Who Controls the Conversation? Social Media and Free Speech."[168] The journal's editors present an unambiguous conclusion: "Free speech on social media is too important to be handled

---

[167] Milton Friedman, *Free to Choose: A Personal Statement*, (New York: Mariner Books, 1990).

[168] https://www.economist.com/weeklyedition/2020-10-24.

by a handful of tech executives." In noting that "societies need solutions today," they recommend that governments "define a framework for obscenity, incitement, and defamation" rather than micromanaging individual posts. They wryly note that Facebook recently removed a comment before realizing that "it was a quote from the Declaration of Independence." Once a government framework is in place, social media executives, "as guardians of the town square," should apply them consistently:

> When societies are divided and the boundary between private and political speech is blurred, decisions to intervene are certain to cause controversy. The tech firms may want to flag abuses, . . . but they should resist getting dragged into every debate. Short of incitement to violence, they should not block political speech. Politicians' flaws are better exposed by noisy argument than enforced silence.

Of course, even with these restrictions in place, social media platforms will still need to set enlightened policies. While decent people can disagree on precisely what might constitute the social media equivalent of crying "Fire!" in a crowded movie theater, platform moderators need to avoid contributing to the "cancel culture" spirit that has begun to intimidate social media users into unhealthy self-censorship, what Duke University professor Timur Kuran calls "preference falsification,"[169] which can invalidate the accuracy of social media data and thus reduce its utility to businesses seeking to serve consumers. Supreme Court Justice Louis D. Brandeis warned, "The greatest dangers to liberty lurk in insidious encroachment by men of zeal, *well-meaning but without*

---

[169] Timur Kuran, *Private Truths, Public Lies* (Cambridge, MA: Harvard University Press, 1997)

understanding."[170] In *The Quiet American,* Graham Greene makes the same point on the destructive sanctimony of the self-righteous Alden Pyle: "I never knew a man who had better motives for all the trouble he caused."[171] In other words, even high ideals can cause disastrous results when mouthed by absolutist activists—whether they come from the public or the private sector, from the right or the left.

No single group monopolizes the threats to free speech on social media. It's become a bipartisan effort. A 2020 letter in *Harper's Magazine* on the growing danger of this trend was signed by writers as varied as former President George W. Bush speechwriter David Frum and liberal iconoclast Noam Chomsky. The letter asserts that:

> The democratic inclusion we want can be achieved only if we speak out against the intolerant climate that has set in on all sides.

> The free exchange of information and ideas, the lifeblood of a liberal society, is daily becoming more constricted. . . . Censoriousness is spreading more widely in our culture: an intolerance of opposing views, a vogue for public shaming and ostracism, and the tendency to dissolve complex policy issues in a blinding moral certainty. We uphold the value of robust and even caustic counter-speech from all quarters. But it is now all too common to hear calls for swift and severe retribution in response to perceived transgressions of speech and thought. More troubling still, institutional leaders, in a spirit of panicked damage control, are delivering hasty and disproportionate

---

[170] Olmstead v. U.S., 277 U.S. 438 (1928)
[171] Graham Greene, *The Quiet American* (New York: Penguin Classics, 2004)

punishments instead of considered reforms. . . . The result has been to steadily narrow the boundaries of what can be said without the threat of reprisal. We are already paying the price in greater risk aversion among writers, artists, and journalists who fear for their livelihoods if they depart from the consensus, or even lack sufficient zeal in agreement.

The way to defeat bad ideas is by exposure, argument, and persuasion, not by trying to silence or wish them away. We refuse any false choice between justice and freedom, which cannot exist without each other.[172]

The signatories focus was largely on the sort of speech restriction that occurs on Twitter and other social media platforms. Perhaps unsurprisingly, even this straightforward and relatively anodyne appeal for a constitutional freedom met with an immediate and angry backlash by the perpetually outraged—on both sides of the aisle.

In his 2020 book *Cancel Culture: The Latest Attack on Free Speech and Due Process,* Alan Dershowitz notes:

Cancel culture is the new McCarthyism of the "woke" generation. . . . And, as with McCarthyism, the impact goes beyond the cancelled individual and affects other members of society, from audiences denied the right to hear cancelled performers, to students denied the right to learn from

---

[172] "A Letter on Justice and Open Debate," *Harper's Magazine,* July 7, 2020 (https://harpers.org/a-letter-on-justice-and-open-debate/)

cancelled teachers, to citizens denied the right to vote for cancelled politicians.[173]

Misuse of social media is the driving force behind these cancellations. The Second Consumer Revolution will achieve its full potential only when consumers feel free to express their opinions on these channels without fear of reprisal.

The Second Right

If the first right is about the freedom to *express* your identity online, the second right ensures that you *own* your digital identity, actions, and behaviors—and can prevent that data from being used without your consent and fair-value exchange. The first right ensures that you are not bullied to falsify your beliefs under the pressure of cultural forces with which you simply feign adherence for fear of being attacked. Doing so may keep the peace, but at the cost of rendering your personal data unreliable for businesses that want to help you discover new products and services. In the terms we introduced in the last chapter, what looks like a meaningful *signal* from the consumer is actually mere *noise*. The result is akin to someone sitting down in a restaurant and ordering an entrée she detests simply because her date insists it's the best thing on the menu. In such cases, the most astute waiter and the most celebrated chef are powerless to offer her any satisfaction. Similarly, someone who enjoys hunting but professes not to (for the sake of avoiding the ire of his animal-rights neighbors) may distort his online profile in a way that limits both his own freedom of choice and the ability of outdoor companies to offer him products he wants (i.e., because his self-corrupted data suggests he *doesn't* want them). The second right ensures that you own your digital identity, that

---

[173] Alan Dershowitz, *Cancel Culture: The Latest Attack on Free Speech and Due Process* (New York: Skyhorse Publishing, 2020)

the honest data you provide is not broadcast indiscriminately to those with whom you would not choose to associate, and that the companies with whom you choose to share this profitable information (e.g., Bass Pro Shops, Cabela's) compensate you for your largesse.

Each social network generates a discrete digital identifier for every consumer that uses their platform. All the actions, preferences, time spent, clicks made, etc. can be and are tracked for each individual digital identification. Your daily digital and online life routine is all recorded, parsed, and categorized for the benefit of advertisers and others who are willing to pay the social networks to reach you, get your attention, try to engage with you, and try to sell you something. That digital identity should be treated like your social security number, your driver's license number, and your credit card number and security code. You give out those numbers when you choose to, when you believe there is a need or value derived from sharing that personal data. Your personal actions, online behaviors, and preferences (your profile), should be your own personal intellectual property. Your activity record and online data should belong to you, so that you are the one to decide how and with whom you interact. Eventually, you should even be able to monetize your personal data and profile. In addition, you should be able to deny access to your digital identification, your personal data, and profile. Today, none of this is the case, and it must change!

The notion that personal data has value is a relatively new concept—in large measure because data analytics tools have only recently made it valuable. Jaron Lanier noted the following in his 2014 book titled *Who Owns the Future?*:

> We've decided not to pay most people for performing the new roles that are valuable in relation to the latest technologies. Ordinary people

"share," while elite network presences generate unprecedented fortunes.

Whether these elite new presences are computer facing services, like Google, or more hidden operations, like high-frequency-trading firms, is mostly a matter of semantics. In either case, the biggest and best-connected computers provide the setting in which information turns into money. Meanwhile trinkets tossed into the crowd spread illusions and false hopes that the emerging information economy is benefitting the majority of those who provide the information that drives it.[174]

Although there was a predictable lag between the recognition of that value by companies as compared to consumers, that interval has ended. As I've emphasized throughout this book, modern consumers are not naive. They are increasingly aware of the value they provide, and increasingly inclined to be compensated for it—whether that be directly through payments or indirectly through convenience, or even discounts.

During his 2019 State of the State address, California Governor Gavin Newsom made this inclination explicit: "California's consumers should be able to share in the wealth created by their data," adding that his team was working on a proposal that would provide a "data dividend."[175] A poll of two thousand registered voters conducted shortly after the speech showed that those who approved of the measure outnumbered those who disapproved by 45 to 28 percent, with 26 percent saying they either needed more information or had no opinion.

---

[174] Jaron Lanier, *Who Owns the Future?*, (New York: Simon and Schuster, 2013)
[175] Marco Della Cava, "California Governor Wants Tech Companies to Show You the Money," *USA Today*, March 10, 2019

I predict that the number of approvers will increase in the near future as the public becomes progressively more aware of the profits their data provides to others.

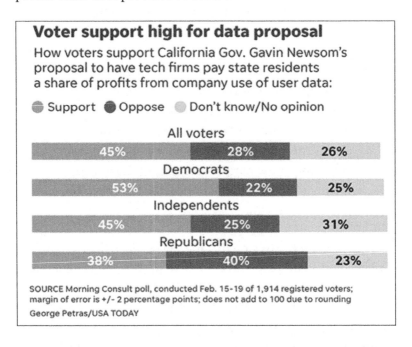

Voter support high for data proposal

How voters support California Gov. Gavin Newsom's proposal to have tech firms pay state residents a share of profits from company use of user data:

● Support ● Oppose ○ Don't know/No opinion

All voters
| 45% | 28% | 26% |

Democrats
| 53% | 22% | 25% |

Independents
| 45% | 25% | 31% |

Republicans
| 38% | 40% | 23% |

SOURCE Morning Consult poll, conducted Feb. 15-19 of 1,914 registered voters; margin of error is +/- 2 percentage points; does not add to 100 due to rounding
George Petras/USA TODAY

Proponents like Lanier argue that this change would be a boon to the overall economy and ultimately serve the interests of both businesses and consumers: "If information age accounting were complete and honest, as much information as possible would be valued in economic terms." He adds that if raw, unprocessed data isn't valued, "a massive disenfranchisement will take place" and consumers' contributions will be unfairly and unwisely discounted. He goes on to say the following:

> In the long term, this way of using network technology is not even good for the richest and most powerful players because their ultimate source of wealth can only be a growing economy. Pretending

that data came from the heavens instead of from people can't help but eventually shrink the overall economy.

Lanier's easoning is hard to dispute:

> The more advanced technology becomes, the more all activity becomes mediated by information tools. Therefore, as our economy turns more fully into an information economy, it will only grow if *more* information is monetized, instead of *less*.
>
> Even the most successful players of the game are gradually undermining the core of their own wealth. Capitalism only works if there are enough successful people to be the customers. A market system can only be sustainable when the accounting is thorough enough to reflect where value comes from.

The Third Right

The third right builds on the second by securing the consumers' right to defend their privacy through encryption and intellectual property (IP) rights. The history of encryption is both mathematically and politically fascinating—going back to Julius Caesar's coded messages to Cicero, Germany's Enigma machine in World War II, Alan Turing's work to crack the Nazi code, Claude Shannon's mind-bendingly byzantine 1949 paper "Communication Theory of Secrecy Systems," and on to the current moment when *Wired* asserts that "mathematicians and computer scientists have developed new algorithms that are sufficiently strong to discourage all but the most determined criminals."[176] Nevertheless, determined (and resourceful) criminals will always be with us—especially when the potential profits from cybercrime are so high. Security companies are not likely to go out of business anytime soon, as they wage an ongoing move-and-countermove battle with highly skilled hackers.

For our purposes, the main import of this battle concerns consumer trust. Early on, many consumers were reluctant to make online purchases because they feared releasing their credit card information into cyberspace. Today, almost all of us make such purchases, and manage our bank accounts online without giving these matters a second thought. Still, improvements are always possible. Although the figures have remained relatively stable, Federal Trade Commission reports show a slight uptick in identity theft and fraud complaints over the last five years. The more fully we guarantee the right of encryption, the greater the capacity of the Second Consumer Revolution to deliver its full benefits to the entire digital ecosystem.

The analogy here is to the ongoing struggle between determined biologists, virologists, and pharmaceutical companies to develop new antibiotics and vaccines in the face of ever-evolving, drug-resistant bacterial mutations, or the emergence of new zoonotic viruses and fungal infections. This isn't a war in which we can ever declare permanent victory since—like those organisms—cybercriminals will continue to adapt to whatever measures we take to defeat them. What we must avoid, however, is an outbreak of deadly digital analogs to MRSA bacteria or the Ebola virus, which, like COVID-19, have the power to shut down an economy. Fortunately, for major issues like identity theft, we have laws to discourage and prosecute human malefactors in ways that don't work against mindless microbial threats.

---

[176] Glen E. Newton, The Evolution of Encryption, *Wired*, (https://www.wired.com/insights/2013/05/the-evolution-of-encryption/)

Moreover, the private sector offers consumers increasingly robust protections. Anyone who listens to podcasts has heard ads from companies like Norton 360 with LifeLock, which—for a fee of $8 per month—promises to protect consumers from criminals who can "file tax returns, steal from investment accounts, or rack up medical bills."

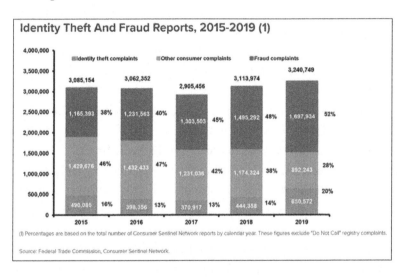

Where we lack protection, however, is in the gray area about who has access to consumer data. My third right would grant consumers the power to have total privacy when they want it—just as business executives do when they enter a boardroom to discuss a new product. Personal data and your personal digital identification should be afforded the same protections by law, treating all of it as your own intellectual property. In addition, if you choose to use encryption methods to protect your data, your communications, your personal preferences, and your profile, you should not be seen or treated as a criminal who's trying to hide your identity or actions from the government.

For SRM to work most effectively, buyers need the freedom to *turn off* their digital identities at any time and to engage through social media channels on a private one-to-one, one-to-two, or one-to-three basis rather than always allowing public access to everything they do with no expectation of privacy.

Consumers deserve a right to selective confidentiality—what they expect when they talk to a doctor or a lawyer. They should be able to share what they want with people they trust, and withhold what they want from those they do not. And consumers shouldn't be made to feel like criminals for wanting this privacy (i.e., What exactly are you trying to hide?) any more than citizens should feel sheepish for exercising their Fourth Amendment rights against illegal searches and seizures by the government. The landmark protection extended in *Mapp v. Ohio* against such intrusions isn't some liberal scheme to protect the guilty. It's a fundamental right of privacy that all citizens deserve—and all consumers.

In his marvelous satirical novel *The Circle,* Dave Eggers pillories those who extend the mindless platitude "information wants to be free" by depicting an eerily overzealous and well-intentioned Facebook-like company that creates a dystopia by insisting that even withholding our most private thoughts from the data gatherers constitutes a social transgression. Relentless video surveillance and corporate invasions of privacy are seen as the cornerstones of social progress, and absurd proponents of this view chant (in lines that would have been at home in Orwell's *Animal Farm*) "Secrets are lies!! Sharing is caring!! Privacy is theft!!" at those with the temerity to challenge the totalitarian status quo.[177] Eggers's book is vital medicine for those who too easily dismiss my contention that allowing consumers to opt out of certain data transactions is vital to a healthy digital ecosystem.

In other industries, like oil or telecommunications, we have licensing requirements that determine who can do what. But in terms of protecting your digital identity or owning your digital presence and your digital actions, there are absolutely no protections whatsoever. It is free game to anybody who can harvest it

---

[177] Dave Eggers, *The Circle* (New York: Vintage, 2014)

and sell it. The only social contract that exists is that by enabling companies to access your data, your digital presence, and your digital actions, you get more targeted, relevant, and contextualized products and services. But that's a very informal, unbalanced protection, and it relies purely on the good business and marketing sense of the sellers. And in a competitive market, that opens the door for some to cut ethical corners and gain a comparative advantage. There is absolutely zero licensing, zero standards set for digital services and data management. I keep asking myself the same question: "How is that possibly correct?" And I always settle on the same answer: "It isn't—not if we want SRM to flourish."

We need to be especially vigilant about those companies that simply gather and sell data without any regard for how it is being used. In an earlier chapter, we looked at the ethical problems that could result if a search engine draws reliable inferences about consumers' health based on their queries and then shares that information with insurance companies rather than with the consumers. That's a separate category from using data to help consumers discover potentially valuable products and services tailored to their interests. In the one case, you're exploiting buyers; in the other, you're acting in good faith to expand their freedom of choice. Clearly, the former requires much more stringent oversight than the latter. That's why we need carefully formulated and enlightened regulatory policies with inputs from consumer advocates, businesses, and government. We don't want just one indiscriminate, heavy-handed set of rules.

In my perfect world, governments, tech firms, and consumer advocacy groups would collaborate to establish farsighted rules. Here, I follow Alan Dershowitz's pragmatic view that we should establish our *rights* based on our shared sense of the *wrongs* we want to avoid rather than on airy visions of unattainable utopias:

> Our collective experiences with injustice constitute a fruitful foundation on which to build a theory of rights. It is more realistic to try to build

such a theory of rights on the agreed-upon wrongs of the past that we want to avoid repeating, than to try to build a theory of rights on idealized conceptions of the perfect society about which we will never agree.[178]

Working in this manner, we can avoid myopic regulations that favor unsustainable short-term ideals over long-term fairness and prosperity.

Recent advancements in AI can be applied to protect consumers and SRM businesses from bad actors and enforce the agreed-upon rules of the road to help keep everyone on the right track. As the nonprofit organization Consumers International advocates, AI needn't be considered a threat, but "the enzyme that rebalances the digital ecosystem."

By working together, we can ensure that we create an environment where emerging technologies are built with consumer safety, privacy, and security in mind. Where digital products and services are as inclusive and affordable as they are innovative. AI is therefore a challenge that consumer organizations can embrace.[179]

The November 19, 2020, cover story of *The Economist* indicates a growing consensus for my third right:

Europe's General Data Protection Regulation (GDPR) is on the way to becoming a de facto standard outside Europe. With closer collaboration

---

[178] Alan Dershowitz, *Rights from Wrongs: A Secular Theory of the Origin of Rights* (New York: Basic Books, 2005)

[179] AI for Consumers, Five Things We Learned at the Euro-Consumers Event on Artificial Intelligence, (https://www.consumersinternational.org/news-resources/blog/posts/ai-for-consumers-blog/)

in intelligence, the alliance could be more alert to security threats from . . . hackers and tech firms. By coordinating their efforts on critical technologies, they could specialize rather than duplicate research. By diversifying supply chains and vetting each link, they can protect themselves from accidental or malevolent disruptions. By working together on technical standards such as Open RAN, which uses mostly off-the-shelf hardware for 5G networks, they can create a favorable environment for their own companies. Crucially, by collaborating on ethical norms over, say, facial recognition, they can protect their societies.[180]

At the end of the day, businesses have more commonality of interest than conflict of interest in maintaining a good, fair, value-driven relationship with consumers. I'm thus optimistic that sellers and buyers can create a secure environment in which both groups prosper in the Second Consumer Revolution.

The Fourth Right

The freedom to choose and to control what, when, where, and how we consume everything and anything has been my focus throughout the previous chapters, so I won't reiterate those points here. My two central tenets are that consumers benefit most from free markets and that modern information technologies provide an unprecedented opportunity to amplify those benefits by allowing businesses to understand, anticipate, and meet consumers' desires with quick, frictionless responses. Equipped with precise information about consumer preferences, sellers are (for the first time in history) able to help buyers discover new products and services

---

[180] "The China Strategy America Needs," *The Economist*, November 19, 2020.

that enhance their lives in ways they could not have anticipated on their own.

My guiding principle has been the collaborative insight of the mathematician John von Neumann and the economist Oskar Morgenstern on the difference between zero-sum and non-zero-sum interactions. In the first, the fortunes of the participants are inversely correlated. The prototypical example is war, in which every advantage for Nation X means a disadvantage for Nation Y. As Nobel Prize–winning economist George Akerlof has shown, when markets are unfree, when unscrupulous sellers hide information from buyers, information asymmetries turn sales into warlike, zero-sum interactions. If I can fool you into buying shoddy merchandise, your loss is my gain.[181]

In non-zero-sum transactions, however, the fates of the two parties are linked. If they cooperate, both parties benefit; if they don't, both suffer. As author and journalist Robert Wright notes, "economic freedom harnesses non-zero-sumness," and throughout history, new technologies have generally increased those freedoms and "expand[ed] the number of people who benefit from the system."[182] Milton Friedman makes a related point in *Capitalism and Freedom*: "There is no law of conservation which forces the growth of new centers of economic strength to be at the expense of existing centers."[183] Friedman adds, "Most economic fallacies derive from the tendency to assume that there is a fixed pie, that one party can gain only at the expense of another. The most important single central fact about a free market is that no exchange takes place unless both parties benefit."

SRM thrives on free-market, non-zero-sum interactions. It is

[181] George Akerlof, "The Market for 'Lemons': Quality Uncertainty and the Market Mechanism," *Quarterly Journal for Economics,* MIT Press, 1970, 84 (3) 488-500

[182] Robert Wright, *Nonzero: The Logic of Human Destiny* (New York: Pantheon Books, 2000)

[183] Milton Friedman, *Capitalism and Freedom* (Chicago: University of Chicago Press, 40th edition, 2003)

at the foundation of The Impatience Economy. The digital age has effectively removed information asymmetries. Given the synergies of 5G mobile, AI, social networks, telecommunications, and rapid distribution channels—fueled by the accelerant of the COVID-19 pandemic. The Social Impatience Economy has the potential to be the most powerful economic force since the Industrial Revolution. Myriad sustainable benefits can accrue to both buyers and sellers—*provided* both parties are free to act in their own enlightened self-interest. In my final section, I'll look at potential threats to that freedom.

The Fifth Right

The fifth right ensures that consumers can benefit from the four other rights, unrestricted by governmental overregulation and capricious corporate policies that curtail basic freedoms. On the corporate side, CEOs looking to cultivate public trust (and if you aren't, you ought to be) should read *Intentional Integrity: How Smart Companies Can Lead an Ethical Revolution,* by Robert Chesnut, former chief ethics officer of Airbnb, which Scott Galloway calls "the most valuable private firm in America."[184] "Technology has created new integrity dilemmas," Chesnut says. "As a lawyer who's worked in public service and in corporations, the evidence is clear to me that proactively addressing these dilemmas is far better than cleaning up the damage they can cause."[185]

Companies who fail to live by Chesnut's code open the door for overzealous government intervention, which typically does more harm than good—however well intentioned. To look at one nightmare scenario, imagine what the government might do if businesses misuse consumer data: legislators could easily step in and declare that every consumer's digital identity must be erased

---

[184] Scott Galloway, "AirbnBaller," *No Mercy, No Malice,* October 16, 2020.
[185] Robert Chesnut, *Intentional Integrity: How Smart Companies Can Lead an Ethical Revolution,* (New York: St. Martin's Press, 2020)

after each transaction. That would certainly solve the misuse problem. But it's the legislative equivalent of burning down your house to get rid of bedbugs. It would leave both businesses and consumers in a pile of bug-free ashes. Unable to form detailed consumer profiles, SRM businesses would falter. And consumers would suffer because, unless those businesses have a personal relationship with them, they can't offer products and services that meet their needs.

Or visualize a scenario in which government decides to limit the percentage of commerce that goes through SRM, so they slap a 20 percent tax on e-commerce transactions as opposed to a zero tax on brick-and-mortar sales. By taking proactive measures, businesses can avoid this kind of encroachment on consumer freedom. As Milton Friedman says, "The role of government . . . is to do something that the market cannot do for itself, namely, to determine, arbitrate, and enforce the rules of the game."

My Digital Consumers' Bill of Rights aims to ensure that the government does this—and nothing more than this. Legislators should determine the rules and consequences, setting the equivalent of the vehicle code that sets the registration requirements, speed limits, vehicle safety requirements, etc. Beyond that, they should step back and let the players perform. They shouldn't be monitoring us or telling us what routes to take to get from point A to point B. The same is true in business. Government should set the framework and then trust the free market to do the rest.

In the last chapter, I'll enumerate fifteen key SRM success points as takeaways from this book that summarize how you can win in The Impatience Economy.

CHAPTER THIRTEEN

Final Thoughts: Who Wins in The Impatience Economy™–and How?

The Moment Is Now!

A HUGE OPPORTUNITY AWAITS INNOVATORS PREPARED TO ride the incoming wave of the Second Consumer Revolution, accelerate into The Impatience Economy, and abandon the backward-looking marketing orthodoxies of the status quo. For the unprepared, that wave will be a tsunami that leaves nothing but wreckage in its wake. Throughout this book, I've given you a view of the massive forces gathering on the horizon and a strategy for harnessing that power rather than being obliterated by it.

If you were hoping I would close with a consoling middle path—a neat resolution saying, "Don't worry; everything will be ok . . ."—brace yourself.

No such path exists.

This is not a fairy tale in which everyone will live happily ever after. Not all flowers will bloom. Refining your old tactics is a waste of time—like trying to build a better horse-drawn carriage to compete with the internal combustion engine. In the post-pandemic landscape, the fatality rate for laggard businesses will be an order of magnitude greater than for those businesses that failed during the pandemic. A significant number of companies have already perished. The tombstones of many more are waiting to be engraved.

Fortunately, yours doesn't have to be one of them. The SRM approach I've laid out will help you take advantage of the new opportunities—the synergies of 5G mobile networks, enhanced AI and machine learning, the ubiquity of social media, the development of rapid distribution channels, and the unprecedented shift in consumer expectations and behavior accelerated by the pandemic.

Those banking on a "return to normal" post-pandemic are in for a rude awakening. As biologist Daniel Pauly points out, whenever change occurs, we experience a "shifting baseline":[186] what was once a luxury quickly becomes a demand. Consumers never revert to old normalcies when change occurs for the better. When you've had an air conditioner, you don't go back to fans. If you gave your sister the latest iPhone last Christmas, she won't be pleased with lavender-scented stationery and matching envelopes this year. When enhancements occur, they become the new baseline, the new normal.

Like God on the sixth day of creation, consumers have looked out upon the face of the newly minted world and seen "that it is good." Your ability to thrive in this new landscape will depend on how clearly you recognize what has changed, how quickly it changed, the benefits implicit in these changes, and how creatively you can expand the range of these benefits beyond what your competitors can deliver.

---

[186] Daniel Pauly, "Anecdotes and the shifting baseline syndrome of fisheries," *Trends in Ecology and Evolution*, 1995.

Key Takeaways: Change Your Mindset; Change Your Business Model

We are past the stage where slight modifications to your business model will be adequate. Those models need to be *entirely* and *rapidly* refashioned in light of the changes I've outlined. The key takeaways from this book are: First, change your mindset, and break the shackles of the status quo so you can see the marketplace for what it *is,* not for what it *was.* Second, you need to focus that new mindset on the following fifteen key SRM success points I've woven throughout the previous chapters.

1. *Speed is essential.* "Buy it now" has been replaced by "Get it now." Impatient consumers expect instant access, instant discovery, instant delivery, instant gratification, instant everything. You need to structure your business the way football teams assess wide receivers: with a premium on speed and agility. The pace is accelerating. You need to keep up.

2. *Marketing 101 won't work.* Forget about traditional approaches. TV, radio, and print are expensive and imprecise. As Galloway says, "If you make your living on the back of thirty-second spots featuring talented actors" and old-school approaches, "this is not the future you were hoping for."

3. *Change the channel.* Consumers spend close to three hours per day on social media. You have access to one-eighth of their day. Your competitors will be taking advantage of this opportunity. You must do the same.

4. *SRM tops Amazon.* History hasn't stopped with Amazon. SRM will make this clear. As of 2020, Amazon Prime had 15.6 *million* subscribers. With social media, you have the potential to connect with 3.8 *billion* consumers. To appreciate that difference, look at the width of your fingernail. That's Amazon's reach. SRM's is six hundred miles.

5. ***Consumers have the power.*** Customers have never had a greater range of choices about what they buy and how they buy it, what they'll tolerate and what they won't. Nor have they ever had greater power to punish or reward a company with a social media post. You can adjust to this new paradigm—or you can line up behind J.Crew, Neiman Marcus, Hertz, JCPenney, Ann Taylor, and the growing list of bankrupt firms.

6. ***Change directions.*** Traditionally, companies would broadcast a one-size-fits-all ad and wait for the consumers to come to them. Today, the traffic pattern is reversed. You have to meet consumers where they live: on social media. If you're waiting for consumers to come to their senses, recognize the obvious superiority of your products and services, and flock to your website, you'll have plenty of free time to start filling out your Chapter 7 paperwork and planning your next career move.

7. ***Relationships precede sales.*** Modern consumers reject overt, unadorned messages that shout, "Buy me!" Businesses need to earn the consumer's trust *before* they display their wares. You can't do that with an infomercial reciting a list of your product's virtues. You must establish an emotional connection with consumers and demonstrate that your values align with theirs. In the long run, you'll benefit from a loyal customer base. Building relationships is the one area of Social Retail Marketing that cannot be rushed.

8. ***Stories and experiences build relationships.*** Taking consumers on a journey, creating a story in which they want to hear more from you—these are the keys to developing trust. How well does this work? Tesla became the most valuable car company in the world during the first six months of the pandemic—more valuable than its next four competitors combined: Toyota, Volkswagen,

Daimler, and Honda—as a result of Elon Musk having made investors feel like part of its "innovation" narrative and having persuaded them to project where the company will be in a decade. This happened even though Tesla will produce four hundred thousand cars in 2020, and the other four companies will produce twenty-six million.[187] Narratives have power. Storytellers make money.

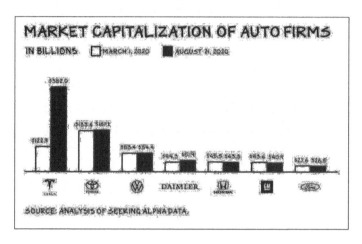

MARKET CAPITALIZATION OF AUTO FIRMS
IN BILLIONS   ☐ MARCH 1, 2020   ■ AUGUST 21, 2020

SOURCE: ANALYSIS OF SEEKING ALPHA DATA

9. **Virtual is the new reality.** On June 26, 2020, Microsoft gave up on physical retail, closing down all eighty-three of its physical stores and switching to online only. "Our sales have grown online . . . and our talented team has proven success [in] serving customers beyond any physical location," said Microsoft corporate vice president David Porter.[188] During the pandemic, Solv Health reported that online doctor visits increased by a staggering 3,339 percent.[189] Daily Zoom meetings increased from ten mil-

[187] Scott Galloway, *Post Corona: From Crisis to Opportunity* (New York: Penguin Random House, 2020)
[188] Shannon Liao, "Microsoft is closing all its stores," CNN Business, June 26, 2020
[189] Heather Fernandez, "The rise of telemedicine: How Covid-19 is fundamentally changing healthcare for all of us," *Solv*, March 30, 2020

lion to three hundred million, a jump of 2,900 percent.[190] More and more people are working from home (saving the average commuter about an hour per day[191]) and ordering food delivery from their phones. Augmented and virtual reality enable us to test products from the comfort of our living rooms. The trend is clear. I predict that SRM will soon account for 80 percent of all sales, and brick-and-mortar sales will shrink to 20 percent. Unless you change your mindset, your customer base will evaporate.

10. ***Friction is fatal.*** The consumer's tolerance for frustration is at an all-time low—and it gets lower every day. Driving to a store, opening and closing multiple apps, dropping a conversation to make a purchase, even negotiating a long series of clicks are enough to cost you a sale. Consumers want the convenience of making a purchase inside their social media feed as they chat with friends. Your ability to meet this need will be crucial to your success.

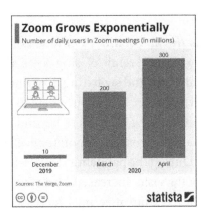

Zoom Grows Exponentially
Number of daily users in Zoom meetings (in millions)

Sources: The Verge, Zoom

statista

[190] Christopher Mims, "The Work-from-Home Shift Shocked Companies—Now They're Learning Its Lessons, *The Wall Street Journal*, July 25, 2020
[191] The United States Census Bureau, (https://www.census.gov/search-results.html?q=Average+Commute+Time+Census&page=1&stateGeo=none&searchtype=web&cssp=SERP)

11. ***Build platform-specific campaigns.*** Your change in mindset is crucial here. You can't simply take your traditional TV and print ads and slap them on social media. You can't even develop a generic social media approach. Instagram isn't Facebook. TikTok isn't YouTube. WhatsApp isn't Twitter. Each platform requires a campaign attuned to the constraints of its format and the preferences of its users.

12. ***Think micro, not macro.*** You can't take consumers on a journey by repeating a one-stop message. A journey requires movement. Traditional ads start and end in the same place. To succeed in the modern marketplace, you need to build hundreds of themes that consistently promote your brand, your philosophy, and your image. Each post should be a stage of a journey that leaves the consumer eager for the next installment—like chapters in a novel. Once you determine your theme, divide it into thirty microsegments that show (i.e., not tell) the consumer the value you are offering. Focus on their cumulative impact rather than a single knockout punch.

13. ***Stop trusting your gut: make data-driven decisions.*** Your gut is a dowser's stick, a divining rod, a vestige from an era that lacked scientific tools. If you rely on a mystical forked stick to find water, you may get lucky now and then. You might survive for a while. But eventually, you'll die of thirst. Data analytics are the business equivalent of hydrologists' seismometers and geologic maps. Part of your new mindset must be a willingness to make tough personnel decisions, replacing your old-school, Mad Men marketing gurus with experts in AI-driven business analytics, digital A/B testing, storytelling, and ever evolving big data insights that help you target and enlarge your customer base and respond to their needs with the specific product variations they most desire.

14. ***Respect consumers' rights.*** SRM is based on trust. Any shortcut you take will squander that trust and jeopardize your long-term success. Once lost, consumer confidence can be difficult or impossible to regain. If you get food poisoning, how likely are you to assume the chef simply had a bad night, and give him a second chance to prove his culinary skills and attention to hygiene? Any unethical behavior will also invite the kind of heavy-handed government intervention that will retard the full flowering of The Impatience Economy.

15. ***Adopt the motto "D-everything" (i.e., digital everything).*** Train yourself to eat, drink, sleep, think, and dream digital. Consumers have drastically changed the way they live and shop. To meet their needs, you need to shift your frame of reference, let go of what worked in the past, and launch yourself into the exciting and profitable future. As Scott Galloway says, if you can do that, "the pandemic has a silver lining that could rival the size of the cloud."

A Call to Action

I'll end this chapter the same way my company—FastForward. ai—ends every SRM journey: with a call to action. You picked up my book because you sensed that your business had entered a period of unprecedented change, that the traditional rules of consumer-producer relations no longer apply. Your instincts were correct. You've read this far because the evidence I've presented has clarified the nature of that change and the consequences of failing to adapt (i.e., business failure). And, if you've read this far, more likely than not, at some or various points of your life you've looked in the mirror and recited at least one positive affirmation to yourself. So here comes your affirmation post-it.

But in case you're not that affirmation person, think of yourself as a philosophy student who has accepted the major and minor premises of a syllogism. All that remains is to deduce the self-evident conclusion:

- Only businesses that adapt *to The Impatience* Economy will survive and thrive;
- My business will survive and thrive;
- Therefore, when I put down this book, I'll embrace the SRM principles and immediately begin to work out how the general rules apply to my specific circumstances.

The logic is irrefutable. Resisting it is futile, a recipe for self-destruction. I am challenging you to accept the reality that Social Retail Marketing is the present and the future, that there is no way to live outside The Impatience Economy any more than you could live on Mars, that the evolving marketplace is going to be bigger than Amazon, and that you need to *act on this insight* with the same impatient intensity that drives your consumers.

The final point is crucial. Simply accepting what you've read as an abstraction is like recognizing that you need an antibiotic to save your life and then refusing to visit the pharmacy to pick up your prescription. I haven't written this book to provide you with knowledge for knowledge's sake. My aim is as practical as the instructions on a defibrillator.

Perhaps in trying to evade my conclusions, someone recently asked me, "What is the penalty for not getting on board with SRM and not accepting that The Impatience Economy is real?" I'll tell you the exact same three words I told her: "Extinction. No exceptions."

I opened this chapter by likening the changing and fluid business landscape to a giant wave rolling toward shore. Mall Store sales have been flat at $150 billion a year since 2000—that's twenty years of no growth. While e-commerce sales have gone from $5 billion in 2000 to $150 billion in 2020. And this is a pre-pandemic image. Project the rising e-commerce slope forward a few years, and ask yourself if you'd rather be riding the crest or sitting in the trough, waiting to be swamped. Those are your choices.

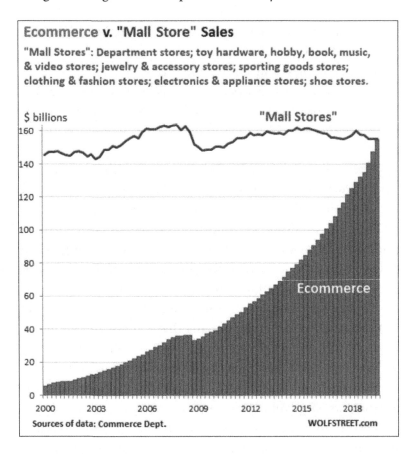

If the stick is being out-of-date and inundated, the carrot is the excitement and thrill of being in sync with the changing times and harnessing the mounting energy to your profit and advantage. Riding the wave can be exhilarating—just as waiting beneath it can be terrifying. If you apply what you've read, you can be a player in a newly dynamic world. If you apply it well, you can be a leader. Francis Fukuyama was wrong when he prematurely announced that the fall of the Berlin Wall signaled "not just . . . the passing of a particular period of postwar history, but *the end*

of history as such: that is, the end point of mankind's ideological evolution."[192] Such end points are always a chimera. If you want to succeed in The Impatience Economy, you cannot think so simply or lack the imagination to see what is yet to come. Heraclitus said the right thing in 500 BCE: "The only constant is change. Nothing endures but change."[193]

Amazon, Facebook, Google, Tesla, and others have earned their place atop the modern hierarchy as a result of the brilliant and innovative work of their founders and teams. But their rise is not the end of history. Insightful and adaptive new companies will eventually challenge and surpass them. Much that we can't yet fully envision will create new opportunities for companies like yours if you are farseeing enough to grasp them. SRM itself will continue to evolve.

My goal is to convince you to aim for where it is going, not for where it is today, and to take full advantage of new financial realities. For example, you can now grow your company without giant investments. You have an unprecedented opportunity to do what we all do as businesspeople and entrepreneurs: make an impact, be seen, be part of that gang of super innovators, be the new Facebook, the new Google, the new Amazon, the new Tesla—because the environment and The Impatience Economy will allow that to happen. And if you develop a mindset capable of meeting this challenge, SRM will give you the entire world as your market. You're not limited to your neighborhood, your zip code, your city, your state, or even your country. You can access the entire world with a few clicks.

In the 1860s, when the world first became connected by the transcontinental railroad, the transatlantic cable, and the Suez Canal, America's greatest and most democratic poet, Walt

---

[192] Francis Fukuyama, *The End of History and the Last Man* (New York: Free Press, Reissue Edition, 2006)

[193] Charles H. Kahn, *The Art and Thoughts of Heraclitus: An Edition of the Fragments with Translations and Commentary* (London: Cambridge University Press, 1981)

Whitman saw what no other writer at the time could see: the power of technology to connect us in triumphant and liberating ways. And though he celebrated these accomplishments—"Singing the great achievements of the present, / Singing the strong, light works of engineers, / Our modern wonders"—he refused to see them as a stopping point.

I'll end with Whitman's potent and poetic call to action—his injunction to put down the book, fulfill your potential, and see beyond the achievements of the present to the grander triumphs yet to come if you are brave enough to seek them.

> *Are thy wings plumed indeed for such far flights? . . .*
> *Passage, immediate passage! The blood burns in*
> *my veins! . . .*
> *Hoist instantly the anchor!*
> *Cut the hawsers—haul out—shake out every sail!*
> *Have we not stood here . . . long enough? . . .*
> *Have we not darken'd and dazed ourselves with*
> *books long enough?*
> *Sail forth! Steer for the deep waters only! . . .*
> *For we are bound where mariner has not yet dared*
> *to go . . .*
> *O farther, farther, farther sail!*[194]

---

[194] Walt Whitman, *Whitman: Poetry and Prose*, (New York: Library of America, 1982)

About the Author

UGIE K FABELA II IS A SERIAL ENTREPRENEUR, PIONEER, and innovator. He is the American founder of VEON, now the world's tenth largest mobile operator, starting with just thirteen team members and growing to a peak of over 60,000 employees in twenty-four countries, with a market cap on the NYSE of over $40 billion. In the course of that journey, he learned a lot about meeting consumer needs, marketing, selling, and predicting where the world was going, which prepared him to write this book.

Augie recognized early the opportunity that the convergence of 5G mobile, AI, and social media offered. The dawn of a new Second Consumer Revolution was clear to him. He left VEON to start FastForward.ai | The Social Retail Marketing Platform™.

Augie holds B.A. and M.A. degrees from Stanford University. He is the youngest Chairman in history of a NYSE-listed company. A world-renowned thought leader and a twelve-year veteran of the World Economic Forum, where he was a founding member of the Community of Chairmen.